CRUCIAL
LAND BATTLES

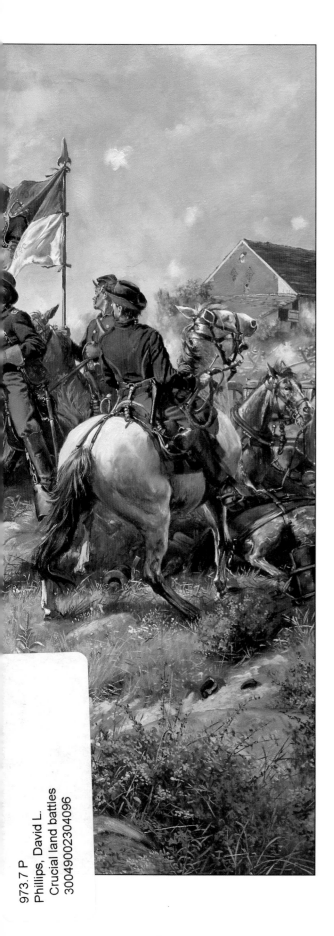

CRUCIAL LAND BATTLES

DAVID PHILLIPS

MetroBooks

MetroBooks

An Imprint of Friedman/Fairfax Publishers

Library of Congress Cataloging-in-Publication Data

Phillips, David L.
    Crucial land battles / David Phillips.
            p.   cm. — (Civil War chronicles ; 1)
    Includes bibliographical references and index.
    ISBN 1-56799-291-9 (HC)
    1. United States—History—Civil War, 1861-1865—
Campaigns. 2. United States—History—Civil War,
1861-1865—Campaigns—Pictorial works.   I. Title.
II. Series.
E470.P447   1996
973.7'3—dc20   95-51983
                                                    CIP

Editor: Nathaniel Marunas
Art Director: Jeff Batzli
Designer: Kevin Ullrich
Photography Editor: Emilya Naymark

Color separations by Bright Arts (Singapore) Pte. Ltd.
Printed in China by Leefung-Asco Printers Ltd.

For bulk purchases and special sales, please contact:
Friedman/Fairfax Publishers
Attention: Sales Department
15 West 26th Street
New York, NY 10010
(212) 685-6610 FAX (212) 685-1307

DEDICATION

There have been three special sources of inspiration for me as I entered into writing: Harriet Phillips, a special grandmother; Natalie Phillips, a special mother; and Sue Phillips, a special and patient wife. Special thanks must be reserved for one who went before: Beuhring H. Jones, who served as a Confederate officer until the fatal day at Piedmont when he and his 60th Virginia Infantry Regiment formed a rear guard to slow a rout and were overwhelmed. Captured and imprisoned at Johnson's Island, he wrote of his experiences in The Sunny Land, a manuscript he smuggled out of prison inside a false compartment in a canteen. Of the study of the Civil War, Jones wrote: "It is a duty we owe ourselves and to posterity, to preserve a faithful record of the events that occurred during that fearful period, and thereby to warn all future generations to avoid the fatal whirlpool of civil contention." This most excellent West Virginia Confederate died while serving as a member of the Constitutional Convention of the young Federal state.

ACKNOWLEDGMENTS

There are many people who have directly and indirectly contributed to my interest in the Civil War. Having lived in a small town that had been under siege by Confederate guns (from a battery where a direct ancestor served), I come by my interest in this subject naturally. But my interest was reawakened by a book called *Civil War in West Virginia*, by Stan Cohen, who has been an inspiration to many writers on the Civil War and whose efforts deserve to be recognized. Additionally, the works of Boyd Stutler, Festus Summers, and Charles Ambler have served as excellent models for works on the subject. Without their efforts, much of the Civil War history of West Virginia might have been overlooked. The fine archives and archivists in West Virginia should be recognized as well. Finally, support provided by Harold Forbes has time and again proven invaluable in several studies I have undertaken, including this one.

CONTENTS

PREFACE

Generation after generation of Americans has developed a fascination with the Civil War since the conflict ended in 1865. A uniquely American war, it was fought in the very yards of many of the members of later generations, who began to study its battles, campaigns, strategy, and participants—almost as if they were preparing to participate themselves. This attraction to the Civil War makes sense: as they begin to undertake research into their family history, members of succeeding generations quickly discover that it was their great-great-grandfathers (and granduncles) who fought the war. These genealogical investigations usually reveal that in most cases it was impossible that all of the ancestors of the researcher living on American soil could have missed service in one army or the other. The discovery of a Civil War soldier in the family tree is always an exciting event, and in some cases the researcher even finds that all eight great-great-grandfathers fought in war.

Ranging from children's fiction to extensive scholarly works, innumerable books are published daily—and have probably been produced at this rate since the end of the Civil War—to feed the insatiable appetite among Americans for information about the war. This particular book is designed to serve as an introduction to the Civil War. The illustrations, many provided by Don Troiani, are lessons in the lives of Civil War soldiers.

The narrative is designed to acquaint the reader with the complex subject of military operations and their direct connection to political outcomes. Large battles were fought during the Civil War as both sides attempted to defeat the armies of the other, but it was not only military victory the combatants sought. Leaders entered into battle with the hopes that the sacrifices made by their men would produce a desirable political outcome. Readers will learn that many of the large, bloody battles of the war were not crucial when the outcome of the war is considered. Instead, the battles that produced the most significant political impact were the most important, and some of these were small and relatively insignificant when the casualty figures are considered.

Fort Donelson in Tennessee was a loss for the Confederates and the first major victory of the war for Ulysses S. Grant. The win secured Kentucky and its large border state populations for the North. Pea Ridge in Arkansas was a relatively small battle, but this Union victory resulted in Missouri remaining under Federal control and ensured that the strategic Mississippi-Missouri River system would be free of Confederate attackers. Antietam in Maryland, another border state, was a bloody stalemate that gave President Lincoln the political confidence to issue his Emancipation Proclamation—an act that precluded potential French and British support for the Confederacy. Gettysburg was

a bloody fight in which Lee's army lost so heavily that it would prove difficult for Lee to engage the Union army in open combat for the remainder of the war. Vicksburg was the scene of a Union victory that resulted in Federal control of the entire Mississippi River, splitting the Confederacy into two sections. Monocacy, also in Maryland, was a small battle in which the Union defenders were able to delay Confederate attackers for a single day, allowing reinforcements to arrive in Washington, D.C., thereby preventing the city's capture (an event that would have cost Lincoln the 1864 election). Peachtree Creek was the battle in the Atlanta campaign in which Confederate defenders abandoned their defensive tactics and attacked Sherman's army in the open, suffering heavy losses that permanently crippled the army. Five Forks was the beginning of the end for the doomed Confederacy: once Sheridan had located Lee's flank and attacked there to break the defensive line at Petersburg and Richmond, it was only a few days until Lee was forced to surrender the Army of Northern Virginia.

These were among the battles that had a political impact and led to a Union victory in a war that threatened to divide the enormous nation forever. This volume is a record of the key events of the war, an opportunity to study the great and dramatic events that served to shape the character of the entire United States.

The Civil War was one of the first conflicts ever to be captured on film. The American public often found the images of carnage too disturbing to view, however, preferring to remember the men as they looked on parade (for instance, this picture of the 7th New York Cavalry).

INTRODUCTION
The Coming of War

The military tasks facing the Federal government in 1861 were considerable because the authority of the National Government had to be reasserted across a very large geographical area—the recently formed southern Confederacy. This enormous region could not be adequately garrisoned to hold the rebelling states in the Union and there were no major objectives that would produce a decisive impact on the morale of the new nation. This rebellion had begun with the seizure by the Confederacy of all of the territory it sought to dominate; in contrast to the complicated task facing Union leaders, the new political leadership of the South had only to defend its territorial boundaries to achieve its political goals.

Northern military strategists were left with no choice other than to establish the Federal government as the aggressor, with the aim of invading and occupying the defended territory of the seceding states. Politically, the role of aggressor was less than desirable: public support, which always runs high for the defense of home and hearth in any society, generally ebbs when a government undertakes an aggressive campaign.

Strategic goals were set for both sides soon after President Lincoln asked for seventy-five thousand volunteers to aid in the suppression of the rebellion. The border states—especially Virginia—refused to become a part of a campaign to attack other southern states

Confederate soldiers began to assemble in large numbers as the winds of war began to blow. Based on volunteer and militia units that had been formed following the John Brown attack at Harper's Ferry, volunteer groups such as this one (Virginia's First Regiment) were made up of men who had drilled and served together— a distinct advantage over their inexperienced Federal opponents.

and eventually seceded. The secession of Virginia was critical in the development of hostilities at this early juncture in what had been, up to then, a bloodless revolution.

Virginia was possibly the most influential state in the country at the time. Nearly one half of the presidents who had served had been sons of the Old Dominion. Many of the settlers who had migrated into newly developed regions in the territories that had become states had originally been Virginians. Proud of their state and its rich heritage, Virginians called the state the "Mother of Presidents" and the "Mother of States." Virginia had a large population, a diversified agricultural system, and levels of industry that could support sustained military operations conducted by large armies in the field. Once Virginia's people had cast their lot with the new Confederacy, the national planners of the South were quick to ensure the Mother of States remained there by moving the capital of the upstart nation to Richmond. Virginia was the key to the rebellion's survival—it gave the rebels the strength that shifted the political and military balance in their favor. Virginia gave the Confederacy a chance for military victory.

Once the stage was set for open warfare, the armies of the North were placed into the uncomfortable role of invader and occupier. The strategic task of the Confederacy was to be that of the defender. One side would invade and the other side would resist. The essentials for Civil War strategy had been set.

The initial strategic planning for the Federal government was conducted by General Winfield Scott, a seventy-five-year-old Virginian soldier who had learned his trade during the Napoleonic period. In the first half of the nineteenth century, however, military strategy had evolved, and up-to-date general principles of warfare had been developed. Younger officers in the national army were skilled in these new approaches to war, but Scott was in command. He began planning the upcoming campaign as if it were an assault on a single fortress, not an entire nation. The initial plan consisted of what was essentially an enormous siege of the Confederacy. Naval forces were ordered into blockade positions and plans were devel-

oped to move armies—once these were raised, trained, and equipped—along rivers in order to divide and seize the South one section at a time. Ridiculed initially, Scott's "Anaconda Plan" would gradually form the foundation of the Union's war strategy.

The most recent military experience of the time had been the Napoleonic wars, series of quick campaigns by large forces against critical positions or smaller forces of the enemy that had resulted in quick, decisive victories. Northern politicians, concerned about the next elections, and younger officers, who were impatient to get into the field, desired a quick war; soon, the Federal army was prepared for offensive action instead of a prolonged siege. The war was beginning as an enormous chess game with the most valuable position on the chess board—in the eyes of the Union army—being Richmond, Virginia, the heart of the South. The strategy to be used was simple: march south approximately one hundred miles from Washington, D.C., capture Richmond, and end the Civil War. The Federal army would encounter the army of the Confederacy along the route as the southern forces attempted to dispute the passage, and a large, decisive battle—similar to those fought by Napoleon—would occur.

Most of the young officers in either army had received training in military tactics while in such military academies as West Point and the Virginia Military Institute. The curriculum included courses in tactics that were derived from the theories of war that had been developed by a Swiss-born officer who had served on the staff of one of Napoleon's marshalls. This man, Jomini, had studied the campaigns of historical leaders such as Napoleon and Caesar and developed practical guides to war planning, and to combat itself. In the United States, Henry W. Halleck, "Old Brains" of the pre-Civil War national army, had analyzed Jomini's writings and agreed that strategy was

Federal commanders General Henry W. Halleck (top), nicknamed "Old Brains" for his scholarly analyses of tactics, and General Winfield Scott (above, seated, with his staff around him) began to plan for offensive operations against the New Confederacy.

simply the art of directing masses to the decisive points of the enemy. Unfortunately, the Confederacy was large and there were no single, clearly defined points that were critical to the survival of the South. In addition, Jomini had identified approaches to be used by forces entering into combat. One of these, "interior lines," shortcuts that afforded rapid troop movement for attack or reinforcement, presented advantages to the army possessing them. In the eyes of Federal planners, the Confederacy had the advantage of interior lines because it was operating defensively while the Union forces were left with the less useful "exterior lines," which rendered the movement of troops to threatened points more time-consuming. The South could move from one threatened location to another after fighting defensive actions more quickly than the Union army could strengthen attacking columns across the exterior lines it was condemned to utilize. The southern defenders were in the best strategic position and there was little the North could do to change this fact.

Major General Halleck's view of national strategy combined with the Jominian requirement for the maintenance of interior lines of communication produced the planning for the first major Federal offensive of the Civil War. The basic principles of war were closely followed as Brigadier General Irvin McDowell concentrated his force of thirty-five thousand men at Washington, D.C. He and the troops then began to move in the direction of Richmond, a decisive point as defined by their most current theory. The planned march of the Union's concentrated force would give them the advantage of the coveted interior lines while forcing their opponents to move against them along exterior lines.

Unfortunately for the inexperienced Federal strategists, a combination of Confederate intelligence operations, railroads that permitted the rapid movement of rebel troops along those exterior lines, and inexperienced Union units and commanders led to a military and political disaster near Manassas, Virginia, on July 21, 1861. This left the Eastern theater of operations in a stalemate from which it was slow to recover. Meanwhile, Union forces were beginning to move aggressively in the West.

The battle fought at Manassas in 1861, Bull Run, was very important and quite bloody, but like most of the Civil War's battles it was not crucial to the outcome of the war itself. Wars are fought for the impact they have on the politics of either side, and the battles that have the most political impact are the most decisive. Large, complex, and violent battles were frequently fought during the course of the Civil War as each army sought to force the other to move into less desirable terrain or to destroy the enemy. These battles, lacking a strong political impact, are more accurately described as "transition battles," during which the armies maneuvered to locate critical points where a future defeat of the enemy would create substantial political damage.

The Confederacy was able to prevail in many of the early transition battles—Bull Run, Wilson's Creek, and Lexington—but Federal forces would ultimately prove the usefulness of Scott's original strategy of utilizing combined army and naval operations under an aggressive commander at Fort Donelson. A second crucial battle would result in a tactical standoff, but a political victory, at Antietam as large armies were assembled and northern manufacturing capabilities were fully mobilized for a long war.

Largely unprepared for the details of a drawn-out conflict, men from both sides of the Mason-Dixon suffered from the effects of the elements during the winters. Here, troops move to bivouac positions in Sibley tents.

Military academies such as West Point in the North and Virginia's Military Institute in the South provided young officers for the new armies. These West Point cadets are graduating into careers that would see differing degrees of glory, death, and destruction.

INTRODUCTION

chapter
1

FORT DONELSON
A Disastrous Blow

Despite the obvious stalemate that developed along hostile lines on the eastern front, Union military operations in the west were far more successful. Winfield Scott, the commanding general of the United States Army in 1861, had proposed to place the entire Confederacy under siege, a gigantic maneuver designed to prevent the export of cotton, which was a principal means by which the rebels raised the funds needed to import arms and war materials. Scott also planned to use Union naval power along southern rivers to penetrate deeply into the interior of the Confederacy and slowly dismember it. Union politicians and the general population in the North, however, were unwilling to agree to a slow, methodical strategy; instead they pressed for rapid victories.

Scott yielded to this political pressure and agreed to attack Richmond in a plan that resulted in the major military and political defeat at Bull Run. This loss and the timidity of George McClellan—the victor in relatively minor, but highly publicized, victories in western Virginia—who replaced the aging Scott, led directly to the stalemate of 1861.

Federal forces in the Mississippi Valley, however, were soon to begin operations against Confederate defenders in the region. Much as Scott had planned, Union naval forces, combined with large Federal military units, began to move along the navigable rivers that extended deep into the Confederacy. The Tennessee River, in particular, offered great tactical advantages to the invaders: it was large, navigable by large steamers, and presented a virtual highway into the undefended rear areas of Confederate forces in both Kentucky and Tennessee. Once this river system was securely held, Union forces could use it as a vast line of communications to deliver supplies and reinforcements as attackers moved toward either the Mississippi River or to the east to threaten Richmond, the newly established Confederate capital.

Previous Confederate defensive measures along the Mississippi system were designed to prevent powerful Union flotillas from accomplishing the much-desired military goal of splitting the enemy (the Confederacy) into two parts. The Confederacy built powerful fortresses at such strategic points as Island Number Ten, Memphis, and Vicksburg to impede any Federal attempts to attack down the Mississippi from the base of operations at St. Louis. In their rush to defend the obvious route of attack, however, Confederate planners neglected the possibility of invasion along the smaller Tennessee and Cumberland rivers.

It was late in November 1861 when serious attention was given to these rivers by both sides. One defensive position, Fort Henry, was hastily constructed on the right bank of the Tennessee River just to the south of Tennessee's boundary with Kentucky. A second, larger defensive position, Fort Donelson, was just as quickly built at a location on the Cumberland River twelve miles away from Fort Henry. Together, these two fortresses constituted the primary Confederate defenses in the region.

Fort Henry was the first to feel the pressure of the Federal offensive. Naval forces—consisting of newly developed ironclad vessels equipped with heavy guns—moved against Fort Henry and managed to force the small garrison to surrender (without the use of infantry support) on February 6, 1861. Most of the defending garrison, however, escaped capture and retreated to reinforce Fort Donelson.

Federal vessels were soon able to graphically demonstrate the military advantage they had gained on the river systems. Three gun-

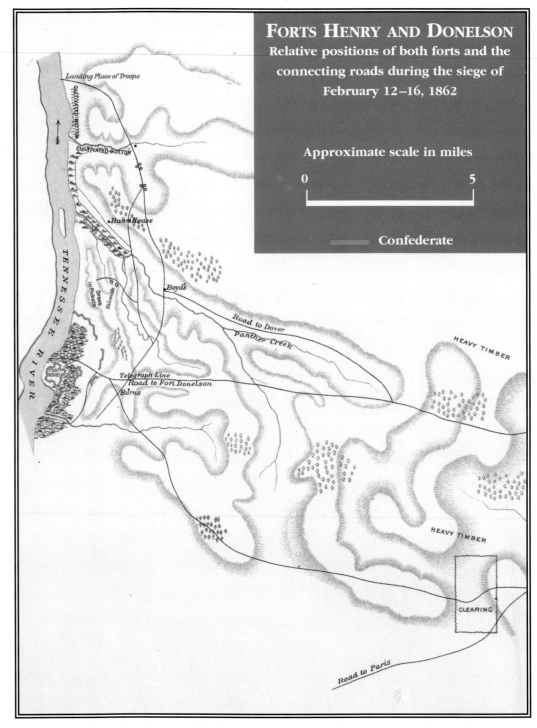

FORTS HENRY AND DONELSON
Relative positions of both forts and the connecting roads during the siege of February 12–16, 1862

Approximate scale in miles

0   5

—— Confederate

Fort Henry and Fort Donelson were hastily constructed as Confederate strategic planners began to realize that combined Federal naval and army operations could penetrate deeply into rebel territory on the rivers. Boats could move fresh Union troops to new attacking points more quickly than the Confederates could march to oppose them.

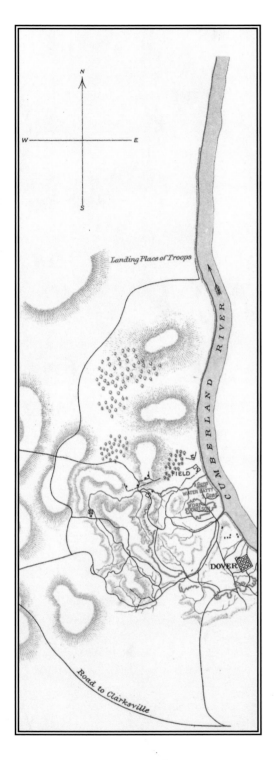

boats moved up the newly opened Tennessee River, past the now-occupied Fort Henry, attacked a vital railroad, destroyed Confederate shipping on the river, and penetrated into Alabama—a state that lay against the Gulf of Mexico. This demonstration showed the danger the defenders were facing as the attacking Federal forces began to gain more and more momentum.

General Albert Sidney Johnston, the Confederacy's regional commander, was placed in an extremely vulnerable position, what with the ability of the Federal navy to conduct unimpeded operations along the Tennessee River, as illustrated by the loss of Fort Henry. There were no defensive positions available to him in Tennessee that Federal forces could not simply bypass to land an army in the defender's rear and then supply them by the river. His defensive line had been easily broken at Fort Henry, and the gathering Union forces could now attack Johnston's remaining forces in Kentucky—at Bowling Green or Columbus—at their leisure. Johnston knew that disaster had

struck and that he must evacuate the forces under his command to new positions below the Tennessee River in Alabama.

The military situation of the Confederate army was complicated by the recent arrival of a new subordinate for Johnston, General P.T.G. Beauregard, the man who had commanded forces at Fort Sumter at Bull Run. The touchy, vain general had quarreled with Confederate President Jefferson Davis and had been transferred to the west. Johnston met with Beauregard in Bowling Green on February 7, 1861, the day after the disaster at Fort Henry. They agreed that there were few options to be considered. First, they could concentrate all of their available forces at Fort Donelson in an attempt to crush the army of Grant, the new fighting general in the Union army. Once this was accomplished, they could shift forces to deal with Buell's army in Kentucky, a separate force that was larger than Johnston's entire army. Second, they could leave a small garrison at Fort Donelson in order to delay the pending attack by Grant as the entire Confederate

Ironclad gunboats, which were relatively new innovations of military engineering, began to appear in large numbers on western rivers. These mobile fortresses could deliver enormous fire power against Confederate defenses and were decisive elements of the Federal attack at Fort Henry.

Defiant Confederate soldiers confidently moved into positions to resist attacks by large numbers of Union troops. Although the Confederate troops were successful in early transition battles, the Union Army's superior numbers and ready access to military supplies and equipment led to a Confederate defeat at Fort Donelson.

General P.T.G. Beauregard was the Confederate commander at Charleston, South Carolina, and ordered the first volley fired in the war, but he proved to be ineffective in the western theater.

army was withdrawn. Remaining in their current location as large Federal armies approached was not an alternative to be considered. The loss of Fort Henry left the Confederate army's lines penetrated and their forces vulnerable.

Curiously, Johnston pursued neither of these options. He was afraid to concentrate his units against Grant because any losses would devastate the entire Confederacy in the West. Rather than assign an expendable rear guard to delay Grant at Fort Donelson, he decided to commit additional troops in an attempt to hold Fort Donelson, a position he feared could be captured by gunboats alone (as had happened at Fort Henry). By the time Grant had closed off the escape route from the fort, Johnston had managed to send

General John B. Floyd, a militarily illiterate for-mer governor of Virginia, was placed in com-mand at Fort Donelson by virtue of his seniority. Under indictment in the North for allegations of fraud while serving in the Buchanan admini-stration, Floyd greatly feared capture by the Federal army.

A former lawyer and a greatly overconfident sol-dier, General Gideon Pillow became second-in-command at the doomed fortress. He had served in the Mexican War, but Pillow knew little about the art of land warfare.

Like the Confederates, the Federal army at Fort Donelson was burdened with politicians serving as generals. General John A. McClernand would be the first to feel the wrath of the trapped Confed-erates as they attempted a breakout. Sherman called McClernan, an ambitious person, "the meanest man we had in the West."

nearly one third of his available strength to Donelson's defense.

Johnston's total force of forty-five thou-sand men had several effective commanders to lead it, but a curious decision was made as to the command at Fort Donelson. Beaure-gard was an experienced combat commander who was available for command duty, but he was sent to manage the withdrawal from Columbus, Kentucky. Major General Hardee, a West Point graduate, was already in com-mand at Bowling Green, but Johnston never-theless went there to assist him with the retreat from Kentucky rather than seeing to it that one of them went to Donelson.

Instead, Johnston allowed three brigadier generals to command within the Confederate fortress rather than assign a major general to

manage them. Senior among these was John B. Floyd, recently Secretary of War in the Buchanan administration and a former gov-ernor of Virginia. Floyd, totally untrained as a military officer, had recently demonstrated his level of military incompetence by mis-managing a campaign against William S. Rosecrans in western Virginia, a series of minor battles and retreats described by Henry Heth as a "comic opera" campaign. This Confederate loss led directly to the cre-ation of a new Union state, West Virginia, in 1863 and was a major political defeat for the efforts of the South to gain foreign recogni-tion. Having been accused of corruption while serving as Secretary of War, Floyd feared indictment, trial, and the "iron cage" in which the Federal army had promised to

display him, if he were captured. This lack-luster brigadier general was senior to the other two generals by virtue of the date he had been commissioned—thus, Floyd was in command at Fort Donelson.

Second in seniority at Fort Donelson was Gideon Pillow, a Mexican War veteran, Tennessee lawyer, and politician. Like Floyd, Pillow was overconfident and poorly suited for command. His commission date gave him the position of second-in-command.

Unfortunately for the officers and men at the doomed fort, the best qualified of the brigadier generals, Simon Bolivar Buckner, was the lowest-ranking brigadier general on hand. He was a West Point graduate—and a personal friend of Grant—who had left the prewar National army to manage his wife's extensive estate in Kentucky. While he was the best of the lot, Buckner had been the last to receive his commission. Their respective dates of rank set the command structure: Floyd was commander of the fort; Pillow, deputy commander; and Buckner, commander of his own brigade.

The fortress was considerably more inspiring than its commanders. Extensive earthworks curved back to rest one flank on the river while the northern end of the works was protected by swamps and a flooded stream. Large artillery positions sited on a high bluff completed the defenses.

Attackers would be moving against Fort Donelson soon. General Grant began to move fifteen thousand men from Fort Henry on February 12, 1862. Unseasonably warm weather induced the troops to discard both blankets and overcoats in the springlike weather. Thus, the Union forces moved quickly, covering the twelve-mile march in a single day, and began investing the Confederate fort by dusk. The perimeter of the Union attackers was large, however, and a large gap was left on the far right of the line. Grant immediately sent for reinforcements that had been left behind to garrison Fort Henry under the command of Brigadier General Lew Wallace. This group of two thousand men was soon marching to close the opening near the river.

Late in the afternoon, the weather began to change dramatically. The springlike conditions of the morning were replaced by sleet as temperatures dropped to 10 degrees Fahrenheit. The soldiers of both sides began to experience what they would later describe as the worst night of the war. Both sides had deployed sharpshooters, and any attempt to build fires attracted bullets. Without fire, all of the soldiers began to feel the effects of the bitter cold.

On February 13, one of Grant's untrained political-appointee brigadier generals, John

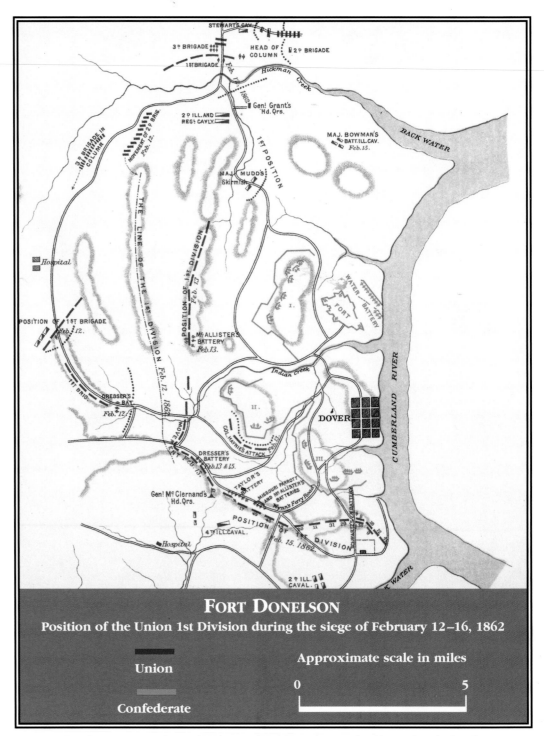

FORT DONELSON
Position of the Union 1st Division during the siege of February 12–16, 1862

Union

Confederate

Approximate scale in miles

0   5

Fort Donelson became a trap for twelve thousand to fifteen thousand soldiers after the breakout attempt of February 12, 1862, failed. Once General Lew Wallace closed off the escape route, the garrison was left with only one option: surrender. Terribly cold weather complicated operations and only a few Confederates escaped capture.

FORT DONELSON: THE FORT AND ITS OUTER WORKS
February 14, 1862

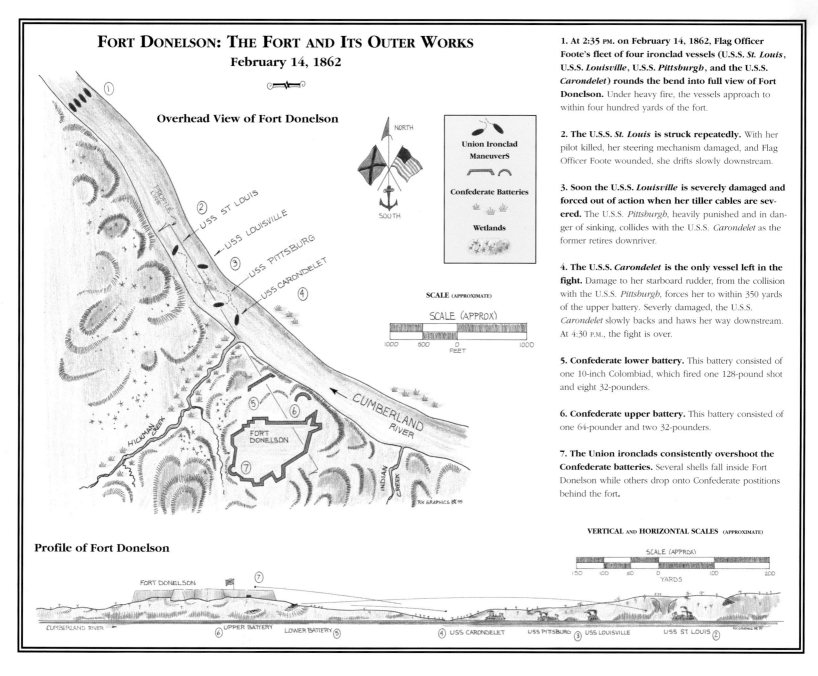

Overhead View of Fort Donelson

NORTH

SOUTH

Union Ironclad
ManeuverS

Confederate Batteries

Wetlands

PROFILE LINE

② USS ST LOUIS

USS LOUISVILLE

③ USS PITTSBURG

USS CARONDELET ④

HICKMAN CREEK

CUMBERLAND RIVER

INDIAN CREEK

⑤ ⑥

FORT DONELSON

⑦

RK GRAPHICS 改 99

SCALE (APPROXIMATE)

SCALE (APPROX)

1000   500   0   1000
FEET

1. At 2:35 PM. on February 14, 1862, Flag Officer Foote's fleet of four ironclad vessels (U.S.S. *St. Louis*, U.S.S. *Louisville*, U.S.S. *Pittsburgh*, and the U.S.S. *Carondelet*) rounds the bend into full view of Fort Donelson. Under heavy fire, the vessels approach to within four hundred yards of the fort.

2. The U.S.S. *St. Louis* is struck repeatedly. With her pilot killed, her steering mechanism damaged, and Flag Officer Foote wounded, she drifts slowly downstream.

3. Soon the U.S.S. *Louisville* is severely damaged and forced out of action when her tiller cables are severed. The U.S.S. *Pittsburgh*, heavily punished and in danger of sinking, collides with the U.S.S. *Carondelet* as the former retires downriver.

4. The U.S.S. *Carondelet* is the only vessel left in the fight. Damage to her starboard rudder, from the collision with the U.S.S. *Pittsburgh*, forces her to within 350 yards of the upper battery. Severely damaged, the U.S.S. *Carondelet* slowly backs and haws her way downstream. At 4:30 P.M., the fight is over.

5. Confederate lower battery. This battery consisted of one 10-inch Colombiad, which fired one 128-pound shot and eight 32-pounders.

6. Confederate upper battery. This battery consisted of one 64-pounder and two 32-pounders.

7. The Union ironclads consistently overshoot the Confederate batteries. Several shells fall inside Fort Donelson while others drop onto Confederate postitions behind the fort.

Profile of Fort Donelson

VERTICAL and HORIZONTAL SCALES (APPROXIMATE)

SCALE (APPROX)

150   100   50   0   100   200
YARDS

FORT DONELSON

⑦

CUMBERLAND RIVER →

⑥ UPPER BATTERY   LOWER BATTERY ⑤   ④ USS CARONDELET   USS PITTSBURG ③ USS LOUISVILLE   USS ST LOUIS ②

RK GRAPHICS 改 99

McClernand, ordered an unauthorized attack against some Confederate gun positions that was repulsed with heavy casualties. Those soldiers who had thought war to be an adventure looked on in horror as some of McClernand's wounded burned to death in brush fires that had been ignited by cannon fire.

On the morning of February 14, Grant was reinforced by Andrew Foote's gunboats and an additional ten thousand men sent by General Halleck in St. Louis. Upon the troops' arrival, Grant immediately ordered attack plans to be made, illustrating how different he was from the generals in the East.

Eastern generals saw the maneuvering of their troops as the primary tactic to force the Confederates into positions where they would have to retreat—allowing the Union troops to capture their objectives—or be destroyed (in much the same way as Napoleon had defeated his enemies in the battles they had studied at West Point). These generals had studied the writings of the Swiss-born strategist, Jomini, and many even carried the master tactician's books with them in the field.

Grant was different. Although he had never read the books of Clausewitz, the Prussian strategist and rival of Jomini—Clausewitz's books were translated into English long after the end of the Civil War—there were large numbers of former German officers in Grant's army who would have known about Clausewitz's aggresive theories of strategy. These theories may have been discussed at some point, as some of Clausewitz's philosophy of combat was apparent in Grant's moves. If this was not the case, Grant knew instinctively that regardless of the central feature of the enemy's power—felt to be the city of Richmond in the East—the defeat and destruction of the enemy's fighting forces is the best way to begin any campaign. Eastern generals chose maneuver and countermaneuver as a means to gain a tactical advantage, but Grant generally chose to attack the enemy's fighting capability when he encountered it.

Flag Officer Foote was fresh from his magnificent victory at Fort Henry and Grant ordered him to move against Fort Donelson. Foote had moved his ironclad boats close to the low water–level batteries at Fort Henry and battered them with heavy cannon until they surrendered. His mobile, iron-shielded batteries had proved to be superior to the earthen, stationary guns at Fort Henry; not surprisingly, Foote attempted to repeat this successful tactic against Fort Donelson. He moved his vessels close to the fort as Grant closed the ring of Federal regiments around the besieged Confederates.

Foote moved his ships to within four hundred yards of the twelve large-bore Confederate guns facing him. Shortly after-

Service aboard the ironclad vessels was not without risk. Any exploding shell that penetrated the gunboats' armor plating would deliver deadly, ricocheting fragments throughout the open interior.

ward, the river began to ring like a blacksmith's forge as solid shot from the fort ripped off iron plating and pierced turrets; a 128-pound shot smashed the huge anchor of the *Carondelet*. Several of the Federal vessels in the small flotilla lost their steering control, crashed into one another, and drifted helplessly away from the fort as the totally unharmed Confederate gunners cheered.

Foote made an error in repeating the tactics he had used at Fort Henry: the gun positions he now faced were placed high on a bluff and he had to elevate his guns to hit these targets. Most of his shots passed over their targets, doing no harm until they fell into the Confederate trenches opposing Grant's ground forces.

This initial round in the battle had gone to the Confederates, but there was little, if any, joy at Floyd's headquarters. The three brigadier generals—Floyd, Pillow, and Buckner—were fully aware by this time that they were caught in a trap that would cost

Indiana provided General Lew Wallace for Federal service. His prompt action at Fort Donelson prevented the escape of the entire Confederate garrison. Later, he would write the popular novel Ben Hur.

them their army if they did not get out quickly. The gunboats would undoubtedly return. The lesson of Fort Henry was still fresh in their minds and they knew it was unlikely that Foote would repeat the error he had just made.

Floyd, Pillow, and Buckner were also aware that Johnston had completed his retreat from Kentucky, freeing them from their rear guard responsibilities at Donelson. They began to plan a breakout.

Their plan was bold and good: Pillow would concentrate the bulk of his forces on the Confederate left while Buckner shifted his regiments toward the center of the line to support Pillow's surprise blow against the thinly held Federal right, near the river where McClernand's troops had moved. Each of the attacking regiments was ordered to carry three days' rations in their haversacks— sufficient food to carry them through the entire attack and escape attempt.

The terrible weather, freezing cold, and howling wind masked Confederate preparations for the surprise attack. Federal pickets and nearby sharpshooters, secure in their knowledge that the siege of Fort Donelson had begun, huddled behind what protection from the elements they could find. They knew they had superior numbers, support from naval batteries, and a fighting commander who was unlikely to relinquish the initiative. They were sure that they would be the attackers when the time came.

Grant left his headquarters before dawn to coordinate his next moves with Foote, now suffering from a wound he had received during the earlier attack against Fort Donelson's batteries. As he left his headquarters that morning, Grant issued orders for all of his subordinate commanders to hold their current positions, preventing any repetition of the unauthorized attack ordered by McClernand on February 13. None of the Federal officers suspected a Confederate

Ironclad gunboats and open mortar boats were capable of delivering a tremendous bombardment against Confederate shore defenses.

assault against them and Grant left the field for his conference with Foote without designating an acting commander in his absence.

Shortly after Grant departed, Pillow ordered his regiments to move out of their trenches. Colonel Baldwin's brigade assumed lead positions in the assault, but his men quickly bogged down as they came into contact with McClernand's men. While they had struck hard at McClernand's right, where the Federal lines were most thinly held, the Union soldiers were not caught sleeping. Most had spent a sleepless night in the terrible cold and were in the act of kindling fires that would not attract the bullets of sharpshooters in the daylight when Baldwin's men struck. Their initial fire stopped Baldwin, but his reserve brigade, composed of recently arrived Virginians under Colonel John McCausland, were rushed forward. These hardy men, fresh from the mountain campaigns in western Virginia, attacked ferociously, and heavy fighting erupted around

the Virginians. The cavalrymen of tough Nathan Bedford Forrest secured the left flank of the attackers and McClernand's men were forced back nearly two miles. The Virginians and Forrest's cavalry had broken through the Federal encirclement, secured the main road, and could now escape. The cost in casualties, however, was high on both sides.

McClernand's men fought until their ammunition began to run out. Panicked and repeated messages were sent for reinforcements, but Grant was still away from headquarters. The meeting with Foote to coordinate their next move had temporarily removed Grant from the scene, and lacking an acting commander, the Union officers at headquarters were unable to make a decision in response to the disaster facing them.

Brigadier General Lew Wallace acted on his own authority to release one of his brigades to go to the assistance of the beleaguered McClernand. Errors were made in the confusion and some of Wallace's men accidentally fired into one of McClernand's retreating regiments, a sorely pressed unit that was fighting hard as it moved under pressure to the rear.

Grant returned to the field at approximately 1 P.M. and quickly took decisive action. (It was at this point in the Civil War that Grant demonstrated his great tenacity and decisiveness, which would prove to be precisely the qualities in a commander for which Lincoln would search in 1864.) Most of the commanders in the Union army at this time would have looked at the disaster facing them and would have pulled their men back into a general withdrawal in this lost battle. Grant quickly collected information regarding the enemy's activities and preparations for battle as he just as rapidly ordered troops forward to recapture the lost positions on the right of the Federal line.

After being advised that captured Confederate soldiers were carrying three days' rations with them, he knew the aim of his opponent was not to defeat the Union army in decisive battle but to escape. Grant knew that the ferocity of the attack meant the Confederates had had to shift large numbers of the men from within the defending earthworks into attack formations, so Grant ordered Brigadier General C.F. Smith to attack the fortress' outer works.

Grant's intuition, decisiveness, and ability as a field commander were shortly to receive some much needed assistance from an unlikely source: General Pillow, who ordered the attacking regiments to return to the doomed fort. The trained soldier among Donelson's brigadiers, Buckner, refused to comply with Pillow's order. The militarily illiterate commander, Floyd, heard Buckner's complaint, and agreed to continue with the breakout attempt, but just as quickly reversed himself after a short discussion with the equally incompetent Pillow. As a result of this confrontation, the attackers gave up the field they had captured at so great a cost and returned to the trenches.

As the Confederates withdrew, Union troops followed closely and were soon in their old positions, which had been lost just that morning. Smith's Union regiments followed Grant's order to the letter as they smashed into the trench line on the Confederate left as the rebels retreated; severe fighting to control the breached defenses began. Buckner attempted to expel Smith's men, but Union artillery had been placed into positions from which they could fire on most of the Confederate soldiers who were counterattacking. With General Smith's men occupying the outer works it became obvious to the three generals that the fort could not be defended.

Floyd, Pillow, and Buckner met a second time at their headquarters to debate their next move. Floyd, untrained and inexperienced, was floundering as a commander just as he had in western Virginia the previous fall and winter. Pillow was equally useless, but both agreed with Buckner that the men lacked the strength to fight another battle.

They called the fort's cavalry commander, Nathan Bedford Forrest, who was surprised that surrender was being discussed. His scouts had located an unguarded (but flooded) road over which the entire garrison could escape. The surrender option was selected, however, as the generals felt the

The end was sealed for the Confederates at Fort Donelson as General Smith's men forced their way into the trenches. Smith shouted, "You volunteered to be killed for love of country, and now you can be!" as his men stormed the Confederate defenses.

men could not survive a march through the deep and freezing waters. Only the choice of commander for the surrender ceremony remained to be decided.

Floyd, the former Secretary of War, had been charged with various criminal actions while in office. Thus, he feared capture, trial, and imprisonment; in fact, he had been the first officer to withdraw from a similar trap at Camp Gauley following a battle with Rosecrans the previous September. He had also led a rapid retreat from a well-planned, but poorly executed Federal trap at Cotton Hill in November. Floyd was excellent in retreat and decided to relinquish command to Pillow.

Pillow, arrogantly overestimating his value to the Confederate war effort, felt the entire Confederacy would suffer a disaster if he were captured. He immediately relinquished command and crossed the Cumberland River in a skiff. Relatively useless, Pillow was the only Confederate officer held in open contempt by Grant.

Buckner, the soldier-officer, would remain in the fort to share the fate of the men under his command. He called for a messenger to carry a message to his old friend, Grant. Meanwhile, Floyd requested permission to escape, once again, from Federal prison—with his Virginian regiments this time. Buckner assented, but with the condition that the escape be completed before the terms of surrender were accepted.

Forrest returned to his cavalry regiment and collected his men. They were going to escape from the doomed fort or die in the attempt. They rode out on the flooded road to safety and many of the cavalrymen carried an infantryman behind him.

Floyd moved his men, two regiments of Virginians and the 20th Mississippi, a regiment placed under his command, to the river bank. Two steamers were approaching the landing at Fort Donelson with loads of

Captain Edward McAllister's Illinois battery moved into positions from where they could fire upon a Confederate artillery position. Conveniently, the recoil from firing these guns threw the gunners and their weapons out of sight of their Confederate targets. McAllister's men fired, recoiled into safety, and then fired again until their opponents' guns were silent.

corn—Floyd would commandeer the two boats and escape with his men. He ordered the men of the Mississippi regiment to secure the boat landing and form a cordon to hold back the deserters and stragglers who were expected to attempt to board the boats in their haste to escape the Union prisons. The men of the 20th Mississippi were also told to hold their positions until ordered to board the boats.

The Mississippians did their duty. Floyd and his Virginia regiments marched aboard the river boats and then left the Mississippi regiment to its fate. Floyd and Pillow escaped the fury of Grant, but they didn't do quite as well with Jefferson Davis, recently a United States Senator from Mississippi. Both were quickly relieved from command for their actions in escaping the fort; only Floyd would receive a

minor command of troops again. Davis never forgave them for their actions at Fort Donelson.

Grant received the note from Buckner, a friend who had loaned him money when Grant had resigned from active service, and quickly considered terms that could be given. After a hasty conference with General Smith, Grant wrote:

Sir;

Yours of this date, proposing armistice and appointment of commissioners to settle terms of capitulation, is just received. No terms except unconditional and immediate surrender can be accepted. I propose to move immediately upon your works.

I am, sir, very respectfully, your obedient servant,

U.S. Grant

Buckner accepted Grant's "ungenerous" terms and was having a sparse breakfast with Lew Wallace when Grant arrived at the Confederate headquarters to accept the final surrender of Fort Donelson.

This was a terrible loss for the Confederates to endure. Grant had captured at least twelve thousand men (and probably more), twenty thousand stand of arms (individual weapons and all associated equipment for each weapon), forty-eight pieces of artillery, the seventeen heavy guns that had held off Foote's gun boats, and large quantities of stores. The Confederates lost over 450 men killed and fifteen hundred wounded against slightly heavier Union losses in killed (five hundred) and wounded (twenty-one hundred).

Unfortunately for the Southern cause, the cost of their loss at Fort Donelson was far greater than the numbers might suggest. The fall of the fort opened the way south into the heartland of the Confederacy and allowed the Union forces to continue with the strategy of splitting the Confederacy along the Mississippi River. More seriously and immediate, however, was the approach of a Federal army at Nashville. As the Confederates evacuated Bowling Green, General Don Carlos Buell moved south from Louisville toward strategically important Nashville. The retreating Confederate army moved through Nashville toward new defensive positions south of the Tennessee River.

Johnston evacuated Nashville and left Floyd in charge temporarily as chaos developed among the city's inhabitants. Soon, Nathan Bedford Forrest arrived and took charge of security: military supplies were saved from looters, food was sent south for the retreating army, and ordinance machinery used in the manufacture of cannon was recovered and also sent south.

Johnston chose to concentrate his forces at Corinth, Mississippi, which bordered precariously close to the Gulf Coast. He could not afford to retreat any farther because important rail lines at Corinth connected vital areas of the Confederacy. Johnston knew that Corinth would become the next critical target of the Federal offensive and he began to assemble forces. There were approximately forty thousand men in Johnston's army by April 1862, when the western Confederates were planning to make their surprise move.

Grant was the man of the hour throughout the North. He became "Unconditional Surrender" Grant in the newspapers, and reports that he went into battle with his cigar led to the delivery of massive amounts of cigars from his admirers. He was very popular at the time—with everyone except General Henry Wager Halleck. Fort Donelson was the largest battle fought in the western theater up to that point, and Grant was shortly promoted to second-in-command, under Halleck, in the western region.

Grant had ranked low in his class at West Point and claimed little understanding of the literature of war. Halleck, "Old Brains" of the prewar National army, viewed himself as an intellectual and would not have been attracted to an officer who lacked similar intellectual qualities. Halleck actually appears to have been jealous of Grant's successes and may have attempted to have kept Grant under wraps as his second-in-command. This had little lasting effect, however, because Grant won battles and had proven the strategy of Winfield Scott—assemble a large army, support it with naval forces, and gradually disassemble the Confederacy—to be sound.

Grant was different from most of his contemporaries, who viewed the Civil War as

Nathan Bedford Forrest, a legendary Confederate calvary commander, led his troops out of Fort Donelson. Refusing to surrender, he and his men rode through deep water and intense cold to make their escape.

a series of battles to be won or lost. He was able to rise above the rest of them, see battles as part of a long series of events, and make the outcome of each individual event—win, lose, or draw—serve his strategy equally well. Here was a general who knew how to fight a modern war, could accept the huge losses of men that resulted from the use of new technologies, and employed new strategies that were being developed to replace those that had been prevalent during Napo-leon's wars in Europe. More important-ly, Lincoln knew he was there and took notice of the new commander and his men in the West.

The impact of the loss of Fort Donelson on the Confederacy was tremendous. Kentucky and territory from which attacks into the North—Ohio, Indiana, and Illinois—could be either threatened or conducted was lost. Tennessee, with its large agricultural capacity and manufacturing capability, was now denied to the South. One of the most strategically positioned of the border states on the western flank, Missouri, was threatened. The Federal forces had proven that their navy could operate successfully on the inland waters: they could attack land positions with heavy guns and deliver battle-ready assault troops and all the necessary supplies, which were being amply produced in the industrial centers of the rapidly mobilizing North.

The new Confederate defensive line was set in the state of Mississippi, resting on the Gulf of Mexico, because Federal gunboats were threatening to split the Confederacy along the Mississippi River. In fact, naval forces were converging from two directions: David G. Farragut's naval squadron was moving north toward the mouth of the Mississippi River and New Orleans, the Confederacy's largest city and principal port, as other gunboats moved downstream to test the South's defenses at Island Number Ten, a fortified position on the Mississippi River.

Albert Sidney Johnston collected all available men in the vicinity to fortify the new defensive line in northern Mississippi as Grant moved forward, waiting for Buell to arrive at Shiloh, Tennessee. Hoping to be able to destroy Grant's army before the arrival of Buell, Johnston and Beauregard attacked the surprised Federal army on April 6. The Union army was steadily driven back,

> *"The blow [Fort Donelson] was most disastrous and almost without remedy."*
>
> *—General Albert Sidney Johnston*

but Johnston was killed and Beauregard suspended active operations a short time afterward. Buell arrived with twenty-five thousand reinforcements and on the following morning Grant regained all of the ground he had lost. The battle was inconclusive, but the Confederates again withdrew to Corinth, Mississippi, and were driven from there on May 30. The Union army now controlled much of Tennessee River, and the Mississippi River, as far downstream as Memphis.

Farragut penetrated the Confederate defenses at the mouth of the river and General Benjamin Butler occupied New Orleans on May 1 as Grant began to plan for operations against the last Confederate stronghold on the Mississippi: Vicksburg.

The taking of Fort Donelson had been the key that unlocked this great series of tactical successes and was one of the most crucial battles of the Civil War.

Federal naval forces continued to press against Confederate strong points. Farragut's squadron soon moved against New Orleans to allow Union troops under General Ben Butler to occupy the city.

chapter
2

PEA RIDGE
Peace for Missouri

A future general, William Tecumseh Sherman had come to the same conclusion as many others regarding the military importance of the rivers of the Midwest. He wrote his brother, John, then an Ohio senator: "Whatever nation gets the control of the Ohio, Mississippi, and Missouri Rivers will control the continent." These western rivers had great length, flowed generally north to south, and reached deep into the heartland of the Confederacy.

The winner in the west would be the side that could control the rivers, but the territories gained through river-borne conquests were really the important strategic targets. The balance of power between the two sides depended on the allegiance or control of two important border states. Kentucky and Missouri were the only slave states beyond the Appalachian Mountains that had not chosen sides, and they could go either way. The outcome of their eventual choice was critical to the balance of power.

The population of either of these two wavering states was larger than any Confederate state except Virginia, and either would greatly increase the military manpower of the South. Their true importance, however, was in their strategic location on the crucial river systems: Kentucky's location commanded most of the Ohio River's drainage, but Missouri was the real prize for North or South to claim.

Missouri dominated the region. If it were a Confederate state, troops from there could block or threaten the Union's major routes between the western states and could threaten southern Illinois. Missouri also controlled a large portion of the Mississippi River, including the vital junction with the Ohio River at Cairo. Clearly, Missouri was a vital strategic prize, and both North and South moved to gain control early in the war.

Neither the Unionists nor Secessionists had any special advantage in Missouri. Many slaveholders hoped to avoid war, and

> "I held the opinion that the immediate possession of the valley of the Mississippi River would control the result of the war. Who held the Mississippi would hold the country by the heart."
>
> —*General John C. Fremont*

PAGE 29: *The intense fighting at Pea Ridge allowed the Union to retain control of the state of Missouri. More important to the longterm military success in the west was the fact that the Union had control of most of the vital Mississippi River. ABOVE: Republican Congressman Frank P. Blair, the son of a trusted friend of Andrew Jackson, was a commander of Unionist Home Guards. Here, Blair (center) and his staff are planning operations against the secessionists.*

Southern sentiment was greatly offset by the recent arrival of thousands of Germanic immigrants who left their homes in Europe after the failure of the revolutions of 1848, which had been intended to establish a constitutional government in a unified country. These liberal refugees had recently taken an oath of allegiance to their adopted country,

the United States, and there was little about the Confederacy that attracted them.

When the Unionists' leader, Frank P. Blair, Jr., a Republican congressman from St. Louis and the brother of Lincoln's Postmaster General, learned of a Secessionist plot to seize the St. Louis Arsenal, he asked for troops to form a guard. Washington sent

eighty men under the command of a tough regular army captain, Nathaniel Lyon, from Fort Riley, Kansas. Blair arranged for Lyon to enlist a large Home Guard to maintain order. Soon the Home Guard came into conflict with the pro-Confederate state militiamen.

On May 10, 1861, Lyon and his Home Guards surrounded the militia camp, disarmed the Confederate sympathizers, and marched them through the streets of the city as a form of public humiliation. Tempers were hot and the Home Guard, primarily German immigrants, were soon being cursed by onlookers. Stones were thrown and someone fired a pistol into the German Home Guard formations. The Home Guard returned the fire. As civilians and innocent onlookers began to fall, the situation became a riot during which twenty-eight civilians lost their lives. This riot and the deaths of the civilians galvanized the citizens of Missouri as perhaps nothing else could have done. All thoughts of remaining neutral were forgotten by the time the funerals were over.

As news of the "massacres" in St. Louis spread, recruits for the Confederacy began pouring into camps and training centers. Command of these new soldiers was given to Sterling Price, a former governor who developed a fixation about winning control of Missouri for the Confederacy. He was joined by fifteen hundred cavalrymen, under Jo Shelby, and fifty-four hundred men from Arkansas under a former Texas Ranger, Ben McCulloch. They soon had a force sufficiently large to turn on Lyon's Union soldiers. By July, Price and McCulloch led a joint command of fourteen thousand men and they moved to attack Lyon. They encamped at Wilson's Creek on August 9.

Lyon planned to hit the Confederates before they could bring their superior numbers against him and made plans with the commander of his German element, Franz Sigel. Formerly a professional soldier, Sigel commanded 1,250 Home Guards, whom he had trained intensively for combat. Lyon and Sigel were making a great gamble in the face of superior numbers.

Sigel was to swing wide to the south, approach the left flank of the Confederates, and strike their rear as Lyon attacked them from the front. Sigel was given an artillery battery to accompany his infantry. Luckily, it began to rain hard and Confederate commanders moved their pickets under cover late in the night. As a result, Sigel was able to get his small force into position without detection.

Lyon's regiments were seen at dawn and they began to advance against Confederate positions on a nearby hill. To the south, Sigel's men waited under cover of trees and began to fire into a nearby Confederate regiment. Unfortunately, Sigel soon made an understandable mistake, but one that cost them their position and the battle.

Sigel wrote that he saw a large number of men in gray uniforms approaching and ordered his men not to fire into them. He assumed these were the men of the Union's 1st Iowa Infantry, ex-militiamen who continued to wear gray clothing. These arriving Confederates, clearly not the 1st Iowa, fired into Sigel's men and charged as the Union soldiers broke in confusion. Sigel made his escape, but the Federal force lost both their positions and most of their cannon—weapons that were turned on Lyon's troops.

The battle ended when Lyon was wounded in the head and then killed by a bullet in the chest. It was an appalling defeat for the Union army, but Lyon's aggressive maneuvering had left the Confederates off balance; furthermore, the Unionists had consolidated their positions in Missouri. Sterling Price was able to occupy Springfield, though his position was weakened when McCulloch took his little army back to Arkansas.

German-born Franz Sigel had emigrated to the United States after participating in the failed 1848 revolution in the German states of the Habsburg Empire. Popular with his immigrant countrymen, Sigel remained in positions of authority in the Union army despite blunders that dearly cost the Federals.

General Nathaniel Lyon was wounded in the head and then killed by a chest wound during the battle of Wilson's Creek.

General John C. Fremont, an explorer of the west and the Republican presidential candidate in 1856, was an uninspiring Union commander in the early battles of the Civil War. He was the first Federal commander to order the freeing of slaves—a political blunder at the time.

Price's next target was Lexington, a large town located between Kansas City and St. Louis. He felt it had strategic importance and moved immediately against the town's small garrison. The three thousand defenders fought without support, little water, and no hope or relief from their commander, former presidential candidate, John C. Fremont, in St. Louis. They fought from earthworks for nine days before surrendering to Price on September 20, 1861.

This second defeat in Missouri, coming so soon after the crushing defeat and death of Lyon at Wilson's Creek, created an uproar in the North. The new prisoners were paroled, but the Confederates kept the hero of the siege, Colonel James A. Mulligan of the 23rd Illinois Volunteers, as a prisoner. Mulligan was held until October 30, when he was

escorted to St. Louis under a flag of truce and released.

Fremont was soon relieved of command, but he did provide one excellent service to his country before he disappeared from St. Louis. He selected Ulysses S. Grant to become the commander at Cairo, Illinois. It was Grant's first major command position.

Little changed in the tactical situation in Missouri for the next few months. Price and McCulloch continued feuding with each other until it became obvious that a new commander had to be found. Colonel Henry Heth, fresh from his personal disaster at Lewisburg in western Virginia (where his numerically superior force had been soundly defeated by George Crook), declined the command. Braxton Bragg also decided his military reputation could be enhanced elsewhere. The

new commander selected was Major General Earl Van Dorn. All of the pro-Confederate Missourians were pleased with the selection of a fighter as their commander.

The Union commander in St. Louis, Major General Henry Halleck, had planned a large offensive against several critical points in the region under his authority. Grant would be sent toward forts Henry and Donelson, Pope would move toward New Madrid on the Mississippi, and a third army under the command of Brigadier General Samuel Curtis would attempt to drive Price from Missouri.

Curtis began to march against Price on February 10. Van Dorn, looking forward to the opportunity to destroy Curtis, sent orders to McCulloch to return with his regiments. McCulloch then sent orders to Brigadier

General Albert Pike to assemble his troops and join him to support Van Dorn.

Pike was leading one of the most unusual armies to march during the Civil War. While he had little military experience, the three-hundred-pound lawyer was an expert on American Indians, and the Confederate government had commissioned the Boston-born Pike to negotiate treaties with the Native American inhabitants of the Indian Territory, today's Oklahoma. Treaties were made with the Chickasaw and Choctaw tribes, but half of the members of the remaining tribes were pro-Union and they moved as refugees into Kansas. The treaties signed with Pike obligated the Confederate Indians to fight only in their territory; likewise, the Confederates were bound by their treaties to come to the assistance of the Indians. Pike was less than pleased with the orders to bring his Indian regiments into Missouri and Arkansas to assist Van Dorn.

A battle raged for nearly nine days as Sterling Price's troops fought for the control of Lexington, Missouri, with the men under Union General John Fremont. His inability to recapture this important population center cost Fremont his command.

General Sterling Price, a former governor of Missouri, was determined to win control of his state for the Confederacy.

Price and McCulloch continued their withdrawal from Missouri into the mountainous territory in Arkansas, where they were joined by Van Dorn. The assembled Confederate army had approximately sixteen thousand men to face Curtis' reduced force of about ten thousand. Van Dorn was confident that he could defeat Curtis and ordered the entire force forward on March 3.

Curtis learned of Van Dorn's approach and moved his men into positions on the north side of Little Sugar Creek, where they began to construct earthworks and field fortifications. In the rear of the positions was a high ridge that had peas growing on vines on its slopes, called locally Pea Ridge. Sigel left a rear guard near Bentonville, fourteen miles away, and engaged Van Dorn on March 6 before falling back to the main body at Pea Ridge. Van Dorn, with little reconnaissance, thought he was engaging the primary Union army and made an attempt to encircle

Sigel, but the German officer was able to extract his men and return to the main force in front of Pea Ridge.

Van Dorn, reluctant to attack the strong positions of Curtis, decided to attempt a maneuver similar to that attempted by Lyon and Sigel at Wilson's Creek. He would divide his forces, attempt to flank Curtis' position, and get into the Federal army's rear area to block any attempted retreat. The coordination of widely separated commands at any time is difficult, but was nearly impossible to achieve during the confusion of a Civil War battle. Van Dorn complicated matters by neglecting to explain his plan to the recently arrived Pike, the commander of the Indian Brigade. The movement began successfully enough, but Curtis quickly became aware of the dual movements and moved large elements of infantry with artillery against McCulloch and Pike as they attempted to get to the Union flank and rear.

PEA RIDGE
March 7–8, 1862

1. The original Confederate plan was to swing behind Big Mountain and attack the Union rear. Aware of this Confederate flanking movement, Union troops block the road with trees and other debris.

2. Slowed by the felled trees, General McCulloch turns his forces around and heads down Ford Road with the intention of joining General Van Dorn's troops near Elkhorn Tavern.

3. As the Confederates approach Little Mountain, Union forces open fire with artillery. The Confederates quickly over-run this position.

4. Confederate forces stop in the woods at the northern edge of a large cornfield. Union forces in the woods along the southern edge of this field open fire. The 36th Illinois advances and drives the Confederates back. Confederate generals McCulloch and McIntosh are killed in this action.

5. A final assault from Little Mountain is flanked and turned by Union forces under General Davis.

6. Around the same time as General McCulloch's initial assault, Confederate forces under the command of General Van Dorn attack Union troops near Elkhorn Tavern. By nightfall Union forces have been pushed back well below the tavern.

7. On the morning of March 8 the entire Union line advances, slowly pushing the Confederates back.

5. By midday, the Confederates are falling back along the Huntsville Road. The Battle of Pea Ridge is over.

Overhead View of Pea Ridge

SCALE (APPROXIMATE)

½   ¼   0   MILES   1

Union and Confederate Forces March 7, 1862

Union and Confederate Forces March 8, 1862

General Troop Movements

Successful Assaults

Failed Assaults

Artillery Positions (Lee Town vicinity Only)

Felled Trees Blocking Road

Spring and Stream

Woods and Open Fields

Profile of Pea Ridge

VERTICAL AND HORIZONTAL SCALES (APPROXIMATE)

SCALE (APPROX)

500   250   0   FEET   500

Confederate General Earl Van Dorn attempted to change the course of the war by capturing St. Louis. A smaller Federal force under General Samuel R. Curtis defeated the Confederates at Pea Ridge and forced Van Dorn back to the Arkansas River. While this engraving shows controlled, orderly soldiers in battle, the Pea Ridge combat was actually a confusing, disorganized affair. Van Dorn's supply wagons had been sent to the wrong position and the Confederates were unable to resupply their men.

Van Dorn quickly realized the danger he was in. His divided force could be overwhelmed, one element at a time, by the now alerted Union commander. Van Dorn quickly complicated matters even further by ordering McCulloch and Pike to reverse their courses. This additional confusion was too much for the commanders to manage. Pike and his Indian Brigade ended up in the rear of a Confederate cavalry brigade commanded by General McIntosh.

Soon the Indian soldiers and McCulloch's troops encountered part of the Union army. McCulloch ordered the attack to begin before the Union commander, Osterhaus, could get

his men in motion. John Drew's Cherokees and a regiment of Cherokee mixed-blood soldiers under Stand Watie forced many of the German soldiers to retreat in panic, but it soon was the Cherokee's turn to be scared as the Union soldiers regrouped and fired shells into their midst. Poor luck began to plague the Confederates making the attempt to get into the Federal rear. McCulloch and McIntosh were killed and Pike suddenly found himself the senior officer on the battlefield. He attempted to set up a defensive line out of the Cherokee and some of the remnants of McCulloch's men, but it was a hopeless endeavor: the men were exhausted. Soon after, Pike

received orders to return to the main body of the Confederate army to support Van Dorn.

Price and Van Dorn had done better with the army's main element and had forced many of the Union soldiers to retreat to the slopes of Pea Ridge. They were winning the battle, but luck intervened in favor of the Union army. Through a serious error, Van Dorn's ammunition train had been sent to positions from which it could not be recalled to replenish the artillery with powder and ammunition. Lacking both food and ammunition, the exhausted Confederates could not consider mounting another attack. The Union artillery began the next morning's engage-

Outnumbered and poorly supplied, Confederate soldiers were frequently forced to scavenge for ammunition from their own dead or wounded comrades. Only through valiant efforts by ordinary soldiers did the Confederacy survive for four years.

> *"[The Battle of Pea Ridge] virtually cleansed the South-west of the enemy, gave peace to the people of Missouri, at least for the next two years, and made it possible for our veterans to reinforce the armies."*
>
> —General Franz Sigel

In the distance, Federal troops advance on the Pea Ridge battlefield to reclaim their former positions at Elkhorn Tavern.

ment and, one at a time, the Confederate guns either ran out of ammunition or were disabled by Union fire. It was March 8.

Curtis brought all of his four infantry divisions into position and ordered a general attack. The Confederates made gallant attempts to hold their positions, but the Union infantry and unanswered artillery began to have an impact. The Confederate left began to come apart as additional Federal infantrymen struck Van Dorn's center, and an orderly retreat quickly became a rout. As with Lyon at Wilson's Creek, the decision to divide his force in the face of the enemy—given the numerous difficulties facing any Civil War commander trying to communicate

with and coordinate his subordinate units during the confusion of combat—had cost Van Dorn the battle.

Pike, angry with the accusations of atrocities that were made against his Indian Brigade and disappointed with the lack of support given him by Van Dorn, simply left the region to return to the Indian Territory. Van Dorn reported that he had not been defeated at Pea Ridge, but he greatly overstated his impact on the military situation in the wake of his retreat.

Curtis had won a major victory for the Union at Pea Ridge. Price and the Confederates in Missouri had won at Wilson's Creek and Lexington, but now this critical state and her large population were firmly held by the Federal authorities. A large part of the Mississippi River was under Federal control and such northern areas as St. Louis, Kansas, Iowa, and the industrial areas of the upper midwest were now safe from Confederate raiding parties. Coming so soon after Grant's major victory at Fort Donelson, the triumph at Pea Ridge gave considerable levels of

comfort to the Union war leaders and their supporters. After Pea Ridge, Missouri remained in the hands of the North for the remainder of the Civil War. And although this border state was to suffer through some of the most severe guerrilla warfare of the entire war (entire counties would be depopulated as a result), in the strategic sense, these ongoing raids were simply a nuisance. Missouri was securely in the grasp of the Union. Price would attempt to invade in 1864, but this would also serve to annoy rather than threaten.

Van Dorn, the handsome, courageous Indian fighter, moved east of the Mississippi and operated there until he was shot dead by a jealous husband in 1863. And Grant was able to turn his full attention from possible threats to Missouri to the campaign against targets in the Mississippi Valley in the continuing effort to split the Confederacy in half.

chapter 3

ANTIETAM
A Bloody, Dismal Battlefield

The war in the east had been proceeding toward disaster for the Union while the northern armies were showing success in the region to the west of the Appalachian Mountains. Scarce resources, inattention from Washington—preoccupied with the threat to the National capital—and relatively weak Confederate forces (when compared to those in the east) under quarrelsome commanders meant that Federal commanders had to react quickly in a creative fashion or face destruction. This strategic situation led Grant to develop a different view of the war than his eastern counterparts. Grant saw the war as a series of campaigns in which losing or winning decisive victories in individual battles made little difference. He realized that if he could hold on to the initiative as he moved to divide the Confederacy along the Mississippi River, he would later have the opportunity to dismember the western Confederacy one part at a time.

This approach was lost on the Federal generals in command in the east. Engagements had been fought within western Virginia as Federal troops moved in an attempt to secure the Baltimore and Ohio railroad, a vital route from the midwest to the eastern seaboard. The first combat death in the war occurred during the night of May 22, 1861, when a small Union reconnaissance team approached the enemy's pickets at the crossing of the railroad with the Northwestern Turnpike. Thornsberry Bailey Brown, a private, lost his life in this skirmish and became the first Union soldier to die. Shortly afterwards, additional deaths would occur in a cavalry skirmish at Fairfax Station. As the casualty lists began to be posted, the attitudes of the opposing sides in the conflict began to harden.

Ohio regiments, under the command of Union General George McClellan, continued to move into the interior of western Virginia

in what became the first maneuver campaign of the war. The first land battle was fought at Philippi in a surprise attack that resulted in a rout of the Virginia state troops encamped there. The campaign continued to develop, and soon battles were fought at Rich Mountain and at Corricks Ford, where on July 13, 1861, Virginia lost the services of an excellent officer, Brigadier General Robert Garnett. (A West Point graduate, veteran of the Mexican War, and recent officer in the National army, Garnett was the first general officer to lose his life in the Civil War.) Meanwhile, McClellan's Ohio regiments were winning small victories inside enemy territory, for which the general immediately came to the attention of President Lincoln.

The first major land battle of the war, however, was fought a few days after Corricks Ford, on July 21, 1861, when Brigadier General Irvin McDowell ordered an army of thirty-five thousand men to advance toward Manassas Junction prior to moving on toward the newly established Confederate capital, Richmond. The bloody defeat of the

PAGE 39: Thrilled by romantic musings about the valor to be won in combat, Federal volunteers such as this young soldier bravely (if somewhat naively) rushed to the service of their country. ABOVE: Federal Teamsters and frightened Union soldiers fled from the defeat at Bull Run in their first "Great Skedaddle." BELOW: Close-order drill was a constant routine in the life of the volunteer soldier. Noise of battle prevented shouted commands from being heard and commanders kept their men in close formations so they could be maneuvered more easily. Unfortunately, rifled muskets soon took a grim toll on these closely packed formations.

Union forces at Bull Run was made possible by the Confederate use of the Manassas Gap Railroad to move their troops rapidly from the Shenandoah Valley. Even if the Union army had been able to win Manassas, however, it is doubtful that the untrained commands and unskilled commanders would have been able to move successfully against Richmond. If they had, it is equally unlikely that the Confederacy would have capitulated (as was widely believed in the North). The city of Richmond, as the strategic point where a loss would be decisive later in the war, had not yet gained the significance later battles would give it.

Soon after the victory at Manassas had given the Confederacy an opportunity to plan for themselves rather than react to Federal movements, a decision was made to send Jefferson Davis' military advisor, Robert E. Lee, to the region of Virginia's western border, along the Ohio River. Lee had been among the most respected officers in the prewar National army and had been personally offered the command of the Federal army by Winfield Scott. But it was as a Confederate commander in the western Virginia mountains that Lee gained his first Civil War combat experience—and this was a dismal failure. Poor weather, mountainous terrain, and quarreling with insubordinate subcommanders (Floyd, Wise, and Loring) rendered Lee's initial campaign a shambles. In fact, it led to a Federal victory that soon after resulted in the creation of a new Federal state, West Virginia.

Lee was accused of incompetence in southern newspapers and he was soon sent on an equally difficult mission. The Federal government had found that Scott's original "Anaconda Plan," which required a blockade against southern ports, was, after all, the best way to win the war. The successful raids against Confederate coastal positions by the Union navy had to be checked, and Davis sent Lee to develop adequate defenses. On the day of his arrival, after reviewing the situation and the loss at Port Royal Sound, Lee decided to abandon the region closest to the sea in favor of new defensive positions to be constructed at points where rivers were narrow, shallow, and defensible. He knew that Federal "floating batteries"—naval bombardment vessels—would be able to defend any infantry landings. The farther inland he could lure the Federal infantry, the less successful the Union's foot soldiers would be without naval gun support. His ability to defend by trading space for time and good positions was sufficiently successful to halt any additional Federal advances in on the coast until Sherman was able to get in the rear of the defenders at the close of the war. Lee proved himself to be an able engineer, and his experience in the construction of field fortifications would serve him well at later points in the war. Lee was beginning to show his military ability—if not genius.

Lee also learned that defensive positions alone were of little value against a large, mobile force determined to capture them. Large numbers, mobility provided by naval transport, and the use of the deadly floating batteries could be used to concentrate overwhelming force against any point Lee chose

Brightly clad Zouaves, men who had been drilled in assault tactics, fought bravely, their units suffering severe casualties during McClellan's Peninsula Campaign. Here, these men are fighting in the Battle of Gaines' Mill.

to defend. This observation would play a significant role in the formation of his later views regarding defensive combat. He was of the belief that the best defense is undertaken offensively.

Lee was recalled to Richmond in March 1862 to return to his post at Jefferson Davis' side as a confidential military adviser. The Confederacy had just lost at forts Henry and Donelson, and their defenses in the west were beginning to break under unrelenting pressure. It was at this point in the war that Lee recommended to Davis that the Confederacy's defensive strategy must be changed. Because the rebel army was always on the defensive, their Federal enemy was able to develop forces capable of attacking anywhere against an army spread so thin that a Confederate victory was unlikely at any location. The best move would be the concentration of their forces and an offensive strategy that would force the Federal commanders to react against Confederate initiatives. Lee continued to urge offensive action, and out of his recommendations came Jackson's brilliant Shenandoah Valley Campaign of April and May 1862. This campaign served the purpose for which it had been designed by Lee: Federal troops were forced to concentrate against Jackson in the Shenandoah Valley rather than serve as reinforcements for McClellan, the primary Federal threat moving against Richmond in what was to become the Peninsula Campaign.

Following the Battle of Seven Pines on May 31, Lee was able to command the Confederate army, rather than recommend and urge; General Joseph E. Johnston, the army's commander, had been wounded, and Davis placed Lee in command. His first order to Jackson was to move his Shenandoah army to the defenses of Richmond to oppose McClellan's army, which Jackson had indirectly weakened through the battles in the Shenandoah and which now was within

hearing of Richmond's church bells. With the addition of Jackson's small army, Lee had approximately eighty thousand men to oppose McClellan's 117,000. Lee, facing a siege he knew his army couldn't survive, chose to attack the larger army of the timid McClellan in what was to become the Seven Days' Battles for the Confederate capital. Both commanders were soon to learn a great deal about the new style of combat.

In order to control and effectively maneuver infantry formations, commanders had to deploy their soldiers in close, orderly assaults or confusion would overwhelm them when they moved beyond the sight of the units along their flanks. Unfortunately for the men who were called upon to fight the Civil War, the development of new rifled weapons and new artillery tactics resulted in terrible losses for the attackers. Lee continued to believe that only with the offensive could the Confederate army survive and pressed the attack against the Union Army at Mechanicsville, Gaines' Mill, and Frayser's Farm before McClellan arrived at an excellent defensive position at Malvern Hill on July 1, 1862. Lee lost an additional fifty-five hundred casualties at Malvern Hill without damaging the Union army significantly.

Lee became the hero of the Confederacy and would remain so forever, but the losses wrought by his new strategy were horrendous. He lost twenty thousand men out of eighty thousand engaged, but he soon moved from the defenses of Richmond to march toward Washington.

He managed the Battle of Second Manassas very well. Jackson's small army held Pope's Union army in position on August 30 while Confederate General James Longstreet's forces moved against the Federal flank, resulting in another rout. In fact, the entire Union army was forced to retreat into the heavily defended environs of Washington. In a curious turn of events that came as

a result of Lee's ability to take advantage of McClellan's timidity, the opposing armies had moved from lines outside of Richmond to lines outside of Washington in less than two months of combat.

This was the general situation as Lee and Davis began to consider their next moves. Lee preferred a continuation of his offensive tactics and recommended an invasion of the North, to be accomplished by entering Maryland. The risks were great because the Federal armies recovering from their recent losses at Manassas would soon outnumber Lee's victorious forces. Lee could have chosen to return to the defenses in the vicinity of the Rappahannock River and wait for a renewed Union attack, but Lee had few doubts about the need to defend Virginia by attacking into the North. The third option that may have been considered at this time was to remain in northern Virginia, but a shortage of food in the immediate area, extended supply lines, and a shortage of transportation made this option untenable.

Lee's reasoning for the recommendation to enter Maryland was relatively sound. Lee contended that he would be able to feed his men and animals on food and forage that would have gone to the support of the enemy while sparing Virginia's farmers the burden of feeding them. The next series of fights with the Federal army would be fought in their own territory—again sparing Lee's beloved Virginia—and the greater part of the Army of the Potomac would be ordered to pursue the invading Confederates, preventing Union forces from planning and provisioning themselves for another attempt to capture the city of Richmond before the end of the campaign season.

Parallel to the military benefits associated with an invasion into Maryland, there were enormous political benefits to be gained for the Confederacy that were considered. Maryland, a border as well as a slave state, had a strong pro-Confederate minority within its borders. Lincoln had only strengthened their resolve early in the war by placing many of Baltimore's pro-Confederate leaders into prison without trial.

The North had managed to antagonize the two European superpowers of the time, Britain and France, and there were diplomatic reports arriving in Richmond that additional political support might be coming. Victories in the North's territory could have served as an impetus for additional European support or perhaps even outright recognition.

There were even reports concerning the growing antiwar sentiments of many of the Democrats in the North. These citizens and the pro-Southern "Copperhead" movement would take comfort in any Confederate successes in the North and there was a possibility that sufficient numbers would enter

General A.P. Hill was given command of one of the finest units in the Army of Northern Virginia, the "Light Division." His men rushed from Harper's Ferry to Antietam to enter the fight without delaying to form lines of battle.

Congress in the fall elections to influence Lincoln and his war party, the Republicans. The war was intertwined with the politics of the period, and the Confederate government hoped to take political advantage of any successes that came its way.

Lee had one additional factor to consider as he and his staff began to make their plans for the invasion. His army was in poor condition after long marches, poor food in limited quantities, loss of excellent officers in recent combat, and poor transportation that would limit the amount of ammunition that would be available in the fighting that would certainly develop. These same soldiers, however, had managed to perform near-miracles in the previous campaigns and Lee was certain they would do so again. They would fight against great odds for the entire war—the Maryland invasion would be no different. Only one real concern remained: the men and their officers had been told that they would only be fighting to defend their homes and states. Would they be willing to participate in an actual invasion of the North?

The Confederacy was rebounding from the battering they had been receiving, primarily in the west, and the autumn campaigns of 1862 showed much promise. Halleck had made a mistake in dispersing his forces in the west and he had over sixty thousand of them spread out in garrisons along railroads from Memphis to Alabama and from Corinth to Colombus, Kentucky. Buell and his army were making repairs on the railroad as they moved in the direction of Chattanooga. This provided Braxton Bragg with an opportunity to reclaim much of the territory lost after Shiloh, but he chose to attempt to recover the state of Kentucky by mounting a new invasion. This was beginning at approximately the same time that Lee was moving into Maryland. Not surprisingly, the North was becoming alarmed over the dual invasions.

South Carolina's Nathan Evans was given the Nickname "Shanks" at West Point because of his overly skinny legs. After graduating in 1848 he was sent to the frontier to fight Indians. He later resigned in order to join the Confederate army, where he served until severely injured in a fall from his horse in 1864.

On September 5, the decision had been made. Lee's headquarters issued orders and the troops began to move to fords in the Potomac near Leesburg, Virginia. The invading army suffered from many deficiencies as it moved toward the Potomac. Many soldiers had not eaten in several days and the prospect of finding food in the immediate future was remote. As many as one quarter of the army was barefoot, and straggling was at record levels. Some of the stragglers were holding back due to personal politics: they had enlisted to defend their homes and did not want to invade the North.

Other problems began to complicate the operation from the start. John B. Hood and Nathan Evans began a dispute over the possession of captured Federal supplies, which resulted in the arrest of Hood for insubordination. A second personal dispute developed between Jackson and A.P. Hill over straggling, and Hill was also placed under arrest. To make matters worse, Lee had been injured in a fall from his horse, Traveller, an accident that resulted in injuries to his hands and forced him to ride in an ambulance as his army spent four days crossing the Potomac near Leesburg.

The news of the invasion spread fear throughout Washington. Recently shocked by the major defeat at Manassas, the Federal government prepared for the worst: clerks were formed into volunteer companies; gunboats prepared to defend the capital; and a boat was prepared to evacuate Lincoln and his cabinet, if that became necessary. Lee had moved into a position from which he could attack Washington, Baltimore, or Harrisburg (a major rail center that was the best of the proposed targets) with relative ease. The Union army commanders began to issue orders to get the Army of the Potomac into motion to check Lee's aggressive moves. The Union was in trouble: Lee was on the doorstep of the nation's capital and Braxton Bragg was massing an army in Kentucky that was threatening to move against Cincinnati.

Lincoln had transferred Pope to the west soon after the loss at Manassas and turned to McClellan. Federal forces were in place at Martinsburg and Harpers Ferry, but their numbers were too small to be able to dispute Lee. Their presence, however, left Lee with a strategic problem that would have to be eliminated if the invasion and subsequent withdrawal were to be successful.

In order to deal with multiple problems simultaneously, Lee divided his already numerically inferior force as McClellan marched to place the Army of the Potomac between Lee and Washington. The Federal commander, as usual, was less than enthusiastic about the need to locate and attack Lee,

Harper's Ferry was the site of a Federal arsenal and the location of John Brown's Raid. Located beneath high hills, the town was impossible to defend from attackers who occupied nearby heights. Stonewall Jackson said he would rather attack it forty times than attempt to defend it once.

General Braxton Bragg was conducting a campaign into Kentucky as Lee moved into Maryland. By October 8, 1862, Bragg was retreating from Perryville after being defeated.

but he was soon to receive the best message delivered to him during the entire war.

Lee had prepared written orders for his commanders on September 9 and copies were made for each of them. On September 13, the 27th Indiana had stopped to rest near Frederick on a campground used earlier by the Confederate army. While resting there, a sergeant and corporal of the Indiana found three cigars wrapped in a piece of paper. Addressed to D.H. Hill, the paper was a copy of Lee's Special Orders No. 191, detailing the plans for the campaign and listing the positions each Confederate commander was supposed to attack. For the first time in the war, McClellan was elated, confident; he wrote to Lincoln that he would "send you trophies."

Harper's Ferry was a clear target whose garrison would have to be eliminated for the Confederate invasion to succeed. Essentially indefensible, the small town was in a deep valley surrounded by high ground. Jackson

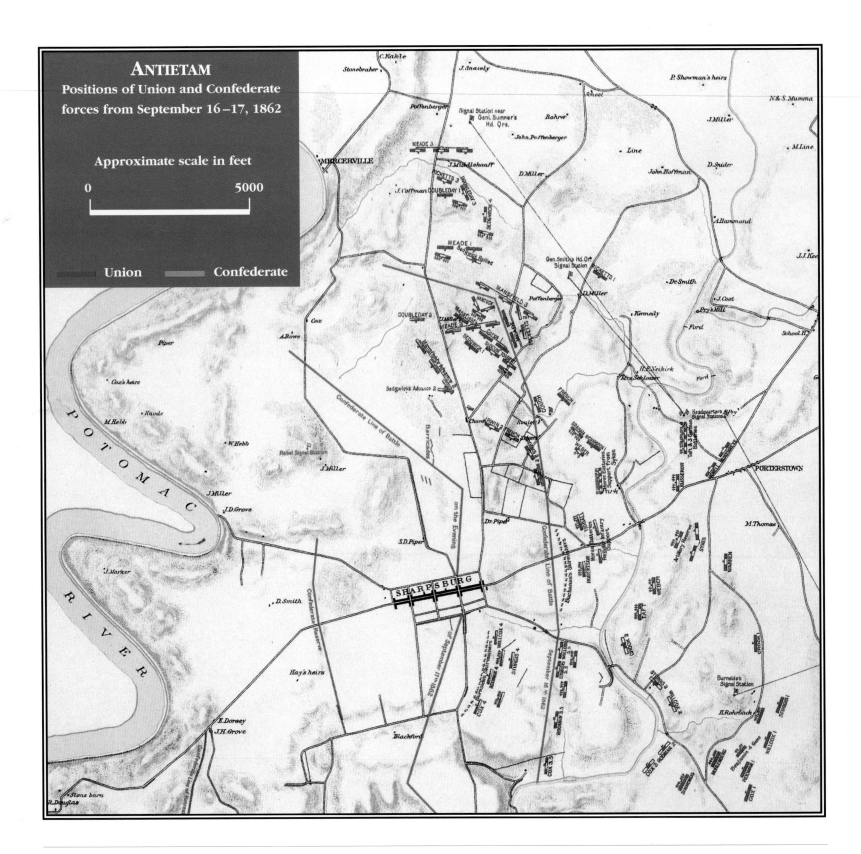

ANTIETAM

Positions of Union and Confederate forces from September 16–17, 1862

Approximate scale in feet

0   5000

Union   Confederate

OPPOSITE: The battle of Antietam was fought piecemeal by General McClellan. Fighting began on the northern portion of the battlefield in the morning, and moved to the center of the field by noon. The fighting continued in the southern portion of the battlefield in the afternoon. Caution on the part of McClellan cost him a clear victory. ABOVE: General Lee, with his aggressive approach, had divided his forces to face simultaneous threats from his cautious opponent. Only rapid marching saved his army from certain destruction after McClellan discovered the lost orders.

commented that he would rather take Harper's Ferry forty times than attempt to defend it a single time; the reasons for this sentiment became readily apparent to the defenders who surrendered to Jackson on Monday, September 15. The Union army surrendered seventy-three pieces of artillery, 12,500 men, and thirteen thousand stand of muskets to the victorious Jackson. There was little time to rejoice, however—Lee sent orders for the separated wings of the army to unite as quickly as possible at the Maryland town of Sharpsburg.

As the battle for Harper's Ferry unfolded, Lee was warned that McClellan had a copy of the lost general order and could

be expected to move with previously unheard-of aggressiveness. An operation to relieve the trapped garrison at Harper's Ferry could be expected; the relief force would probably cross South Mountain in the vicinity of Boonsboro, Maryland, at gaps in the mountain, particularly Turner's Gap. Lee sent orders to Longstreet, who was near Hagerstown, to move to defend the gap against a certain Federal attack.

Simultaneously, the Kanawha Division of the IX Corps, under an able commander, Jacob D. Cox, had the lead position as the Federal army approached South Mountain. Cox and his men, toughened by long service and hard marches in the mountains of western

Virginia the previous year, marched swiftly without straggling, but halted when they encountered a familiar figure standing beside the road.

The lone officer, Augustus Moor, had recently been captured by the Confederates near Frederick and had just been paroled. He was making his way back to Federal lines. When Cox told him that their destination was Turner's Gap, Moor forgot for a moment that the terms of his parole prevented him from providing information. A hasty comment, "My God! Be careful," was all that escaped his lips, but Cox was warned. He sent a dispatch to IX Corps Commander, Major General Jesse Reno, a West Point graduate from Wheeling, Virginia, to warn him of the enemy presence on South Mountain.

Severe fighting erupted, but Cox was able to control Fox's Gap by late morning. The cost in lives was heavy (future president Rutherford B. Hayes was severely wounded during this engagement). Cox moved his men toward Turner's Gap, but the arrival of reinforcements for the thin Confederate line delayed Cox and he returned to his position at Fox's Gap. The arrival of reinforcements for both sides led to a general and fierce engagement, with additional combat developing at nearby Crampton's Gap. South Mountain had gradually become the scene of a major battle.

Reno rode out on a commander's reconnaissance late in the evening in an attempt to find a weakness in the Confederate defenses that could be exploited, and was severely wounded in the process. As he was being carried to the rear, the brave Reno announced firmly and cheerfully to one of his division commanders that he was "dead," and soon died of his injury.

The day ended with the Federal army holding the high ground at South Mountain. Lee decided to pull back to positions near Sharpsburg. The news from Jackson that

ANTIETAM

48

OPPOSITE: Terrible casualties were suffered by both sides in the frantic combat to control a twenty-acre field of ripening corn that was adjacent to the Hagerstown Pike. It is remembered in military history simply as "The Cornfield." ABOVE: The romanticism associated with warfare was eliminated from American imaginations after they viewed Alexander Gardner's photographs of Antietam's dead. The terror of the Civil War was driven home to the average citizen by images such as this one of dead Confederates along the Hagerstown Pike.

Harper's Ferry had been captured arrived late on Monday morning. Lee elected to fight McClellan at Sharpsburg, Maryland, though his force would be dangerously small until Jackson arrived. Preparations were made to fight the battle along tree-lined Antietam Creek. Excellent defensive terrain favored the Confederates and a road running north-to-south would allow the commanders to move troops swiftly from one position to another once the battle had begun. There was one dangerous feature of the selected battlefield: the defenders would have their backs against the broad Potomac River and could thus be destroyed if the battle went completely

against them. Lee was the only general in the Southern army who would have been willing to fight a battle against superior numbers from a position such as this. Above all, Lee was a combative general—and he knew his opponent's tendency toward timidity.

As predicted by Lee, McClellan brought his divisions into position slowly. The first arrived in the afternoon on Monday, September 15. He finally arrived in person during the afternoon on Tuesday, September 16, but by then a great advantage had been lost. Three divisions of Jackson's troops had arrived, significantly reducing the numerical advantage held by the Union army. The

stage was set for fighting that would surely develop the next morning, September 17.

Amazingly, McClellan ordered a series of separate, piecemeal attacks against Lee's army that Wednesday morning. If he had attacked with the entire force available to him, the Army of Northern Virginia would have been severely defeated. Given the proximity of the Potomac in the Confederates' rear, it is unlikely that very many of them would have escaped capture. A grand opportunity was being squandered along with the lives of many excellent Federal soldiers. Attack after attack across pastures and cornfield against the Confederate left flank was turned back. McClellan next ordered attacks against the center of the Confederate line, but these division attacks also met with a bloody repulse. Entire regiments were decimated in a hail of minié balls and canister. The 12th Massachusetts entered the fight with 334 men, and emerged at the end of the battle with just one hundred of them.

Similar losses resulted among the Confederate army. The Louisiana Tigers, a fierce elite regiment, marched to Sharpsburg with approximately five hundred men, but left 323 of them behind after only fifteen terrible minutes of combat. Jackson's divisions had a large gap smashed into them and their line was about to break when John Bell Hood's division, denied their breakfast by the order to attack, stormed forward and slammed into Hooker's I Corps. Nearly one third of Hooker's men would be killed or wounded as the corps was effectively taken out of the battle. Hood's losses were also horrible to contemplate; many of his men fell to Federal artillery batteries that had been double-loaded with canister before being fired into the Confederate line. Later, John Gordon's men gave their lives to help defend Sunken Road, a feature of the local terrain that would be renamed "Bloody Lane" as a result of their sacrifice.

The focus of the battle shifted to the Federal left flank, where Ambrose Burnside—through a mistake in orders—shared command with Jacob Cox, the officer who had opened the attack at South Mountain. The valor of the men of Cox's Kanawha Division would be rewarded shortly by Burnside, who gave them the honor of opening the attack on a bridge over Antietam Creek. Three Ohio regiments from the Kanawha Brigade under George Crook were selected to carry the bridge. His attack went wide, missing the approach to the bridge. A second attack also failed. McClellan, growing impatient with the repeated failures, sent a message to Burnside that he was to take the bridge "if it cost him 10,000 men." A third attack was sent forward through the hail of bullets from the defenders on the opposite side. A Georgia brigade held its position at the bridge, pulling back at the last possible moment when the company ran short of ammunition.

McClellan saw a ray of hope for the first time that day. The plan of breaking Lee's northern flank had been abandoned and all of the attacks along Sunken Road were slowing to a halt. The advance across the bridge was the single option remaining—thus, what had begun as a bloody diversion became the focus of Federal strategy. Orders were sent to press forward, but the lead regiments were short of ammunition. Couriers were sent to get reserves to replace the exhausted men who had fought their way across the hotly contested bridge. Burnside continued his buildup along the creek and Lee realized the peril he was in. His final chance to salvage the battle rested with the long awaited arrival of A.P. Hill and his Light Division, one of the best units in the Army of Northern Virginia. The recall order arrived at Hill's position at Harper's Ferry early that morning and he had been relentlessly driving his men toward Sharpsburg. By 2 P.M., Hill's men were crossing the Potomac at Boteler's Ford

General Longstreet described the Confederate dead in their positions in the Sunken Road as, "Mowed down like grass before the scythe." The road became immortalized as Bloody Lane forever.

Union troops pushed to cross this bridge over Antietam Creek. It would be named after Federal commander General Ambrose Burnside.

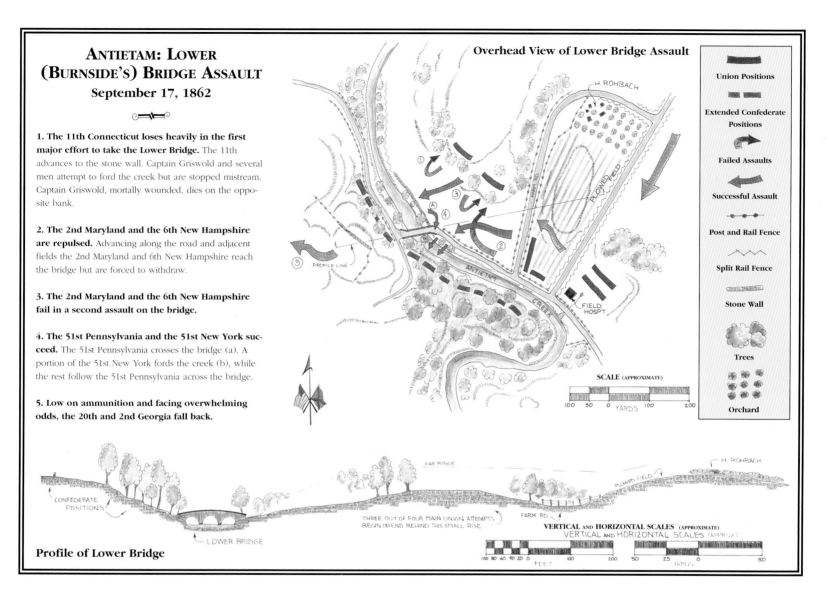

ANTIETAM: LOWER (BURNSIDE'S) BRIDGE ASSAULT
September 17, 1862

1. The 11th Connecticut loses heavily in the first major effort to take the Lower Bridge. The 11th advances to the stone wall. Captain Griswold and several men attempt to ford the creek but are stopped mistream. Captain Griswold, mortally wounded, dies on the opposite bank.

2. The 2nd Maryland and the 6th New Hampshire are repulsed. Advancing along the road and adjacent fields the 2nd Maryland and 6th New Hampshire reach the bridge but are forced to withdraw.

3. The 2nd Maryland and the 6th New Hampshire fail in a second assault on the bridge.

4. The 51st Pennsylvania and the 51st New York succeed. The 51st Pennsylvania crosses the bridge (a). A portion of the 51st New York fords the creek (b), while the rest follow the 51st Pennsylvania across the bridge.

5. Low on ammunition and facing overwhelming odds, the 20th and 2nd Georgia fall back.

Overhead View of Lower Bridge Assault

Union Positions

Extended Confederate Positions

Failed Assaults

Successful Assault

Post and Rail Fence

Split Rail Fence

Stone Wall

Trees

Orchard

SCALE (APPROXIMATE)

100 50 0 YARDS 100 200

Profile of Lower Bridge

VERTICAL AND HORIZONTAL SCALES (APPROXIMATE)

100 80 60 40 20 0 FEET 100 200

50 25 0 YARDS 50

near Shepherdstown. They had covered fifteen miles in slightly over six hours. Two miles remained, however, between the Light Division and Lee's forces.

Time was short. Confederate defenders were being badly mauled by large, relatively fresh Union regiments and the thin line of defenders was coming apart. Hill's Light Division arrived just in time and didn't stop to form lines of battle. They began fighting as they spread into their customary battle formations and drove back the Federal attackers. Burnside had lost 20 percent of his corps, but he still had more than twice the number of men on the field as did the Confederates. Overcome with doubts, Burnside began to wonder whether he could hold the hard-won bridge, and asked McClellan for reinforcements that would not be sent.

Curiously, the cautious McClellan had the battle won, but he did not know that success was in his immediate grasp. He had two corps in reserve and, if he had had the nerve, these fresh regiments could have been thrown forward into the thinly held Confed-erate battle line, which would have been destroyed. He lacked the resolve to throw his last reserves into the battle, however, and lost a grand opportunity to permanently seal the fates of the Army of Northern Virginia, Robert E. Lee, and perhaps the entire rebellion.

One man out of every four engaged had been killed or wounded in the battle fought along the banks of Antietam Creek.

The indecisive engagement, one of the turning points of the entire war, left the opposing forces facing one another on the morning of September 18. The losses of the previous day were the greatest that had occurred in American history: 22,726 men had been killed or wounded.

Lee marched for the safety of Virginia that night—the first invasion of the North had come to an end. McClellan, predictably, refused to attack even though two fresh divisions arrived to reinforce his army, giving the Union commander a two-to-one advantage. McClellan had had enough combat and Lincoln had had enough of McClellan, who was relieved of his command. Little "Mac" reviewed his troops for the last time on November 10 and began to prepare to run for president, opposing Lincoln as a peace candidate.

While the battle at Antietam had technically been a draw, Lee's repulse from northern territory gave Lincoln the opportunity to issue the Emancipation Proclamation. This document would have a great impact far from the area in which the Civil War was being fought. Lincoln had hoped to deprive the Confederacy of much of its economic strength by encouraging many of the South's slaves to escape, but the greatest impact of the Proclamation was felt in Europe.

Britain and France had been waiting to decide on recognition of the Confederacy, but the Emancipation Proclamation's moral impact in countries where slavery had been forbidden long ago ensured that the Confederacy would fight alone against the North. There would be little discussion of foreign help after the battle of Antietam. Lincoln carefully constructed his proclamation to liberate slaves only in the states in open rebellion against the national government. The border states, which were slave-holding areas, could still choose to join the rebellion and Lincoln carefully avoided offending

TOP: Soldiers under the command of General Joseph Hooker attacked Confederate formations near the Dunker Church. Entire lines of men were killed by aimed volleys from either side. ABOVE: This artillery caisson and dead soldiers mark the final position of Hooker's doomed advance.

President Abraham Lincoln met with General McClellan after the bloody fighting along Antietam Creek. Although it was a military stalemate, the Battle of Antietam presented Lincoln with an opportunity for a major moral and political victory: the issuance of the Emancipation Proclamation.

them. This partial liberation of slaves was met with some degree of anger as Lincoln's message seemed to be that someone could not own another human being—unless he was loyal to (or at least neutral toward) the United States during the Civil War. Then, as now, it was impossible for a politician to please everyone.

The tide had shifted favorably once again for the Union. Lee had been repulsed in Maryland and on October 8, Braxton Bragg was driven from Perryville, Kentucky, by Buell. Northern armies had been battering

> *"It was never my fortune to witness a more bloody, dismal battle-field."*
>
> —General Joseph Hooker

the defenses of Richmond in June and July and Lee had won a brilliant battle at Manassas at the end of August, but by October the fortunes of war had shifted once again (at Antietam).

Grant began repairing the mistakes that had been made by Halleck and was busily concentrating his forces in the west for a drive on Vicksburg in an effort to secure for the Union the whole length of the Mississippi River, thereby splitting the Confederacy and denying Richmond precious resources from the Confederate West.

chapter 4

VICKSBURG
Flowing Unvexed to the Sea

The Federal army had been doing well in the west after their Confederate opponents had returned to widely dispersed positions and a static defense—the curse of the defender who is responsible for securing every line—following their frustrated counteroffensives at Shiloh and Perryville, Kentucky. General Joseph E. Johnston, now recovered sufficiently from the wounds he had received at Seven Pines, returned to the field. This excellent commander, however, lacked the resources to be able to halt Federal operations as Grant continued to maneuver toward his well-defined strategic goal, the opening of the entire length of the Mississippi River.

Command of the Confederate forces in northern Mississippi was assigned to Lieutenant General John C. Pemberton, commander of weakened forces too widely scattered to be able to resist the concentrated attack Grant was planning. The key to the control of the river was the city of Vicksburg, located on top of a bluff two hundred feet above the river.

Heavy guns on the high bluff located on a great bend in the Mississippi were positioned where they could dominate river traffic for miles in either direction. The lessons learned by naval officers at Fort Donelson would not be repeated here. The powerful batteries and extreme range that the guns of Vicksburg were capable of covering made this bend in the Mississippi a very dangerous place for an attack.

Combined operations conducted by Federal forces on the Mississippi drainage had experienced considerable success up to this point in the war. Farragut and Butler had captured New Orleans in spring 1862; Memphis—the northern extreme of the Confederacy—had fallen in June of the same year. The South still held Vicksburg and Port Hudson, however, along with the 250 miles of the Mississippi River that lay in between the two strongholds.

Lincoln, as any good chief executive would, had defined the military objective in

> "If it should be asked why the 4th of July was selected as the day for surrender, the answer is obvious. I believed that upon that day I should obtain better terms."
>
> —General Joseph C. Pemberton

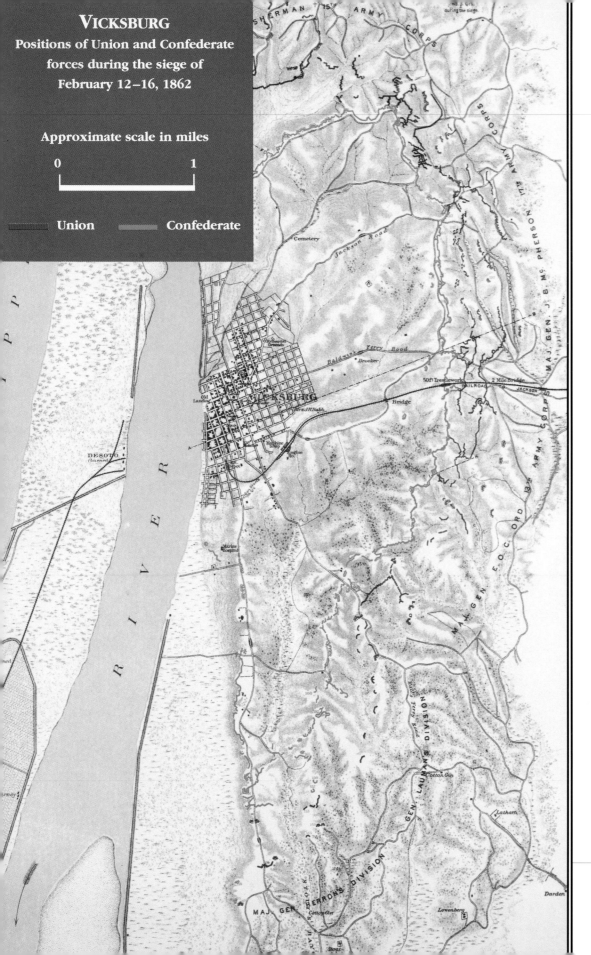

VICKSBURG

Positions of Union and Confederate forces during the siege of February 12–16, 1862

Approximate scale in miles

0   1

Union   Confederate

PAGE 55: Federal naval schooners were able to shell Confederate shore positions with newly installed mortars. These large, heavy weapons fired shells high enough into the air that they plunged vertically into the entrenchments at which they were aimed. LEFT: The decisive point of the Confederate defensive along the Mississippi, the critical transportation route for the South, was the city of Vicksburg. General Fremont had claimed that the side "controlling the Mississippi Valley would win the war." Knowing that the loss of the crucial rail and river shipping that went through the city of Vicksburg would threaten the existence of the Confederacy, Grant began to move to claim the fortress city.

grand terms: the Mississippi River should "roll unvexed to the sea." The success of this campaign would yield far more than the symbolic and political results suggested by Lincoln's words. With the securing of the Mississippi, the Federal military would be able to deny the Confederate East the supplies and thousands of reinforcements from the rich states of the Confederate Southwest. Vicksburg was the key—if it should fall, Port Hudson could not be defended.

The strategically important city could have been occupied easily at any time in early 1862, but Van Dorn had been ordered there soon after the battle at Pea Ridge. Since June, fifteen thousand of Van Dorn's men had been busily digging defenses and constructing field fortifications on the heights. Vicksburg was rapidly becoming the "Gibraltar of the West."

Federal troops, gunboats, and vessels carrying large siege mortars began to arrive along the Louisiana shore opposite Vicksburg, and troops were landed to begin to fortify the area. Engineering officers quickly recognized the obvious strength of Vicksburg and suggested a plan to bypass the fortress without a costly battle.

Vicksburg was located at the tip of a large, narrow bend in the river; plans were

made to dig a new channel for the Mississippi through the narrow neck of the peninsula. Soldiers and laborers, many of them African Americans, continuously worked on the canal while Farragut's floating batteries shelled the city's defenses from the river in an unsuccessful attempt to silence the defender's batteries. Farragut raced his vessels past Vicksburg's guns on June 22 and was joined upstream by additional gunboats from Memphis on July 1. Naval engagements against the strong shore batteries continued, but July 1862 was not a good month for the Federal forces.

Halleck was soon promoted to command in Washington, and Grant assumed command in the west. Pemberton was assigned Van Dorn's command in Vicksburg in October

TOP: Prosperity came to the river city of Vicksburg after taxpayers subsidized the construction of railroads linking it to distant markets. ABOVE: The Warren County Courtroom, with its Greek-styled columns, dominated the view of Vicksburg from the river. Steamboats delivered goods and produce to the city's wharves and warehouses, where they were stored until freight cars could move the items to the interior of the Confederacy.

Union forces under General William S. Rosecrans battled Braxton Bragg's Confederates to a bloody draw at Murfreesboro, a battle that took place early on in 1863.

"*A proper use of the available resources of the Confederacy would have averted the disasters.*"

—*General Joseph E. Johnston*

as Grant placed Sherman in charge of a thirty-two-thousand-man army, which moved quickly to attack the city's defensive lines at Chickasaw Bayou on December 20. Pemberton was able to rush reinforcements to the bluffs above Sherman's large army and the ensuing battle cost Sherman two thousand casualties while the Confederates lost fewer than two hundred men.

December was a month filled with additional reverses for Grant's men. Nathan Bedford Forrest, one of the escapees from Fort Donelson, raided deep into the north of Grant's army and cut the Union army's telegraph communications and destroyed nearly sixty miles of railroad.

Van Dorn's Confederates had also been active; they raided the Federal supply depot at Holly Springs, capturing fifteen hundred

men and $1,500,000 worth of military supplies. Grant was left without supplies and communications for eleven days as he marched northward to Grand Junction, Tennessee, a distance of eighty miles. Grant only learned of Sherman's defeat at Chicka-saw Bayou, the third of December's reverses, on January 8, 1863.

There was some good news for the Union in December, however, following the standoff between General William S. Rosecrans and Braxton Bragg at the battle of Murfreesboro. This battle, a strategic defeat for the Confederacy, cost Bragg twelve thousand men he could scarcely afford to lose as he was forced closer to Chattanooga.

Grant's reverses were taken in stride as he continued to keep his general objective in view. Lost battles did not mean the end of a

General Joseph E. Johnston, convalescing from a wound he had received at Seven Pines, had left Robert E. Lee in command in Virginia and could spare no troops for the defense or relief of Vicksburg after Grant began his siege.

Very heavy casualties resulted from the Federal attack on Fort Beauregard, a part of Vicksburg's defenses. The color-bearer of the 22nd Iowa Regiment may have planted his colors on the high breastworks, but the attackers were driven back.

VICKSBURG

campaign and Grant continued to press toward Vicksburg with his usual tenacity. Other plans failed and rising water destroyed the channel intended to allow Federal ships to bypass Vicksburg's guns, but these failures only served to increase Grant's determination to capture the fortress.

Grant's next moves were more successful. Gunboats and transports protected infantry regiments that were delivered fresh (i.e. not exhausted by days of marching prior to entering battle). Sherman was sent on a diversion against the doomed city's defenses in late April as Grant prepared to move on a fast-paced campaign into the interior of Mississippi.

Abandoning his base and supply depots at Grand Gulf, knowing that Pemberton could be expected to move against his nonexistent supply lines back to the river, Grant moved out on a three-week campaign inside hostile territory. His gamble permitted his troops to operate on the dry land south and east of the city while his troops lived off the land as they maneuvered between the forces of both Pemberton and Johnston. As anticipated, Pemberton moved to cut Grant's abandoned supply lines with the river rather than unite his forces with those of Johnston to strike Grant in a decisive battle. This error allowed Grant to wage a maneuver campaign between the forces of his two enemies over which he would have had no numerical advantage if they had united their forces. Grant's losses were slight, and within three weeks Vicksburg was completely invested by

ABOVE: While Grant's army attacked Vicksburg from land, the Union navy shelled the town from the Mississippi River. Federal naval officers had accepted the risks associated with sailing their ocean warships into the shallow waters near Vicksburg. RIGHT: The Union navy played a decisive role in securing various waterways important to the Confederacy and shelling strategic cities along southern and western rivers.

VICKSBURG
61

VICKSBURG
62

OPExPOSITE: *The 8th Wisconsin Infantry and mascot, an immature bald eagle named "Old Abe," rush into withering fire during the siege of Vicksburg.* ABOVE: *The artillery at Vicksburg turned out to be useless because defenders were unable to lower their muzzles sufficiently to draw a bead on the Union attackers.*

Union besiegers. His army had marched 180 miles, won five battles, captured Jackson, Mississippi (the state capital), and caused six thousand Confederate casualties.

Grant ordered a general assault on the defenses of Vicksburg by his entire army on May 22, 1863, but the attack failed. The Federal army settled into a general siege: trenches were dug, tunnels were dug beneath the defenders and exploded, and by July 1 the Confederate garrison was using the last of its resources. Vicksburg raised the surrender flag on July 3, and on the following day, the nation's birthday, Pemberton and his sol-

diers surrendered. The "Gibraltar of the West" had fallen.

As predicted, Port Hudson was unable to continue to resist Bank's attacks and the entire garrison surrendered three days after Vicksburg capitulated to Grant. July 1863 was the beginning of the end for the Confederacy. Vicksburg's defenders had ceased to resist on July 3—the same day the final shots were fired at Gettysburg.

Grant had demonstrated his ability to successfully manage his army through military reverses that would have halted other generals in their tracks. He had shown that he was willing to gamble for high stakes when he abandoned his base of operations and entered a maneuver campaign for three weeks inside enemy territory. His excellent Mississippi campaign served as a model for Sherman in the latter's triumphant march through Georgia to the sea. Grant

had proven that the risky project of maneuvering behind enemy lines could be handled successfully.

Losses for the Confederacy were enormous following the fall of Vicksburg. Nearly thirty thousand officers and men surrendered, giving up 172 artillery pieces and approximately sixty thousand muskets. More seriously, the Mississippi River was now open to Federal navigation from New Orleans to St. Louis. The Confederacy had been dealt a near-mortal blow. The new nation had been split, denying the East large quantities of supplies from the West. At the same time, the possibility of recognition from Britain and France was more unlikely than ever following major Union victories and the Emancipation Proclamation. The Union was winning on both military and political fronts.

"Port Hudson surrendered because its hour had come. The garrison was literally starving. With less than 3000 famished men in line... what else was left to do?"

— Lieutenant Colonel Richard B. Irwin

General John C. Pemberton served as the Confederate commander at Vicksburg. He came under suspicion from other Confederates because he had been born in Pennsylvania. After marrying a woman from Virginia and serving in the South with the prewar national army, he came to love the region.

chapter 5

GETTYSBURG
Pitting Force Against Force

Following the general standoff between Lee and McClellan at Antietam in September 1862, McClellan was replaced by General Ambrose Burnside. The new commander of the Army of the Potomac returned to the old strategy of invading Virginia, which brought the opposing forces together at the Rappahannock crossings, near Fredericksburg. Lee's army fought a purely defensive battle there from protected positions that allowed the Confederates to receive Union assaults and decimate them. Lee won a lopsided victory at Fredericksburg and would have been well advised to remain in prepared, fortified positions to repel additional invasions as they came. Gradually, the will of the northern population to continue the attack at such a high cost in lives lost might have been sapped. The logic, however, that had led Lee to attempt the invasion of Maryland in 1862 was still active.

Lee had managed to win some decisive victories, but the Union was continuing its

advance in the Mississippi region and the naval blockade was beginning to draw tighter daily. He continued to feel that recognition by the North and peace for the Confederacy could be achieved only through large-scale military victories within northern territory. As Lee saw it, the South could win the war only by breaking the political will of the northern population to continue fighting; and this would never happen if Federal reverses occurred only in Virginia. He also knew that eventually Federal success in the west would permit large Union forces to shift against the Army of Northern Virginia and eliminate it.

Before he could prepare for a second invasion, however, Lee was forced to send Longstreet and his three divisions to southeast Virginia and North Carolina's coast to counter a potential amphibious landing that would threaten the railroads connecting North Carolina and Richmond. If Lee had not been forced to send Longstreet south, it is

> "Gettysburg was the turning point in the great struggle.... [It] inspired the armies and people of the North.... [It] was at Gettysburg that the right arm of the South was broken."
>
> —General E. M. Law

PAGE 65: *General George G. Meade and the other Union commanders of the Army of the Potomac assemble following the Battle of Gettysburg. Their victory resulted in a greatly weakened Army of Northern Virginia, a Confederate force that would be unable to return to offensive operations after their losses in Pennsylvania. OPPOSITE: The men of the Army of the Potomac demonstrated incredible courage and devotion to the Union: the Irish Brigade suffered enormous losses during the battle of Fredericksburg and yet the survivors were willing—even anxious—to continue fighting. RIGHT: The Confederate army had advantages—higher positions to shoot from and stone walls to conceal them—in their efforts to devastate the attacking Federal regiments at Fredericksburg. The lopsided Confederate victory should have served as a model for future operations, but the aggressive Lee went over to the offensive and struck into Pennsylvania.*

likely that Lee would have opened the 1863 campaign season with an invasion of Pennsylvania. As it was, Lee and his diminished army remained in position near the city of Fredericksburg.

Following the battle of Fredericksburg, Burnside had been replaced by Major General Joseph Hooker, who managed to surprise Lee with an aggressive crossing of the Rappahannock at the end of April. Lee immediately ordered Longstreet to return with his three divisions, but these were so dispersed that they could not be recalled quickly enough.

Hooker ordered his army to swing wide to the west to avoid the Confederate defenses at Fredericksburg, which had caused the dramatic losses in Burnside's attack in December. The circuitous approach gave Jackson an opportunity to make a rapid march and a flanking maneuver against the Federal right. The Federal army, though defeated initially in this attempt, fought hard and reestablished good defensive positions, but Hooker ordered a retreat—back across the Rappahannock.

Lee's sixty-thousand-man army had managed to defeat a force that was twice as large, and they had accomplished this dramatic feat while Longstreet's three divisions were absent from the field. Unfortunately for the South, the great Stonewall Jackson died during this engagement (at the Battle of Chancellorsville), which was a great military and personal (for Lee) loss, but Lee was beginning to believe that his Army of Northern Virginia was capable of accomplishing any task he set before it. On May 9, Longstreet rejoined the army at Lee's Fredericksburg headquarters, and by June 3 the Confederates were preparing for the long march north.

Lee met with his cavalry commander, Major General James Ewell Brown (Jeb) Stuart, near Culpeper, Virginia, at Brandy Station on June 8 and inspected Stuart's five brigades of cavalry. Nearby Federal cavalrymen, eleven thousand strong, attacked early the following morning in what was to become the largest cavalry battle ever fought

on the North American continent. The battered Federal cavalry performed well against the more skilled Confederates and developed confidence in their abilities for the first time in the war.

Stuart paused to repair the damage the fighting had inflicted on his troops, but Lee would wait for nothing. He ordered General Richard Stoddert Ewell to move on June 10, the day after the battle at Brandy Station, in a new, skillfully planned campaign. Ewell marched through the Shenandoah Valley toward Winchester as Longstreet moved on a parallel course on the eastern slope of the Blue Ridge Mountains. A.P. Hill was ordered to follow Ewell's route once Hooker's army began to move. Ewell had only recently been assigned to command Jackson's corps, but he would pass his first test with flying colors.

By June 13, Ewell's lead divisions were approaching Winchester, where Federal Major General Robert Milroy commanded a garrison of over five thousand men. Both Lincoln and Halleck had been trying to convince Milroy of the wisdom of a rapid retreat from Winchester to the (albeit dubious) safety of Harper's Ferry, thirty miles away, but Winchester's commander felt he was safe, particularly since the Army of the Potomac would prevent the enormous Confederate army from moving rapidly against him. Realizing his error as the attack began, Milroy ordered an evacuation during the night, but encountered a large force that had been sent to block his retreat.

A general engagement opened that night at Stephenson's Depot, approximately four miles northeast of Winchester, and by dawn Milroy's small army had suffered 443 casualties and lost 3,358 prisoners to Ewell's corps. The opening battles of the 1863 campaign had gone well for the Confederates, and the long, gray-clad columns continued their lengthy march to the Potomac crossings. Curiously, they would make the move without the scouting of much of Stuart's cavalry.

Stuart had received severe criticism in the Richmond newspapers following the surprise Union attack at Brandy Station. Given his flair for the dramatic, everyone expected him to recover some of his reputation in the upcoming campaign. Stuart wanted to harass Hooker's troops. Lee reluctantly agreed to the plan, but insisted that the cavalry move to the left flank of the infantry columns as soon as Hooker crossed the Potomac. Stuart's best brigades moved out on June 25, and from that point on through much of the upcoming battle they were unable to provide information to Lee as to the location and movement of Hooker and the Army of the Potomac.

Uneventful crossings occurred at the Potomac, and the Confederate army marched into the interior of Pennsylvania. On June 27, Lee learned while he was at Chambersburg—from a report from Longstreet's scout Harrison—of Hooker's move out of Maryland and across the Potomac. He gave orders to have the Army of Northern Virginia concen-

ABOVE: General Joseph Hooker was given command of the Army of the Potomac following Burnside's defeat at Fredericksburg. Soon, however, he was defeated after a fierce battle at Chancellorsville and George Meade replaced him. OPPOSITE: After winning at Chancellorsville, Lee began to move his army into Pennsylvania in order to locate food and supplies. Their marches would culminate at the small town of Gettysburg.

trate its forces to meet Hooker's army because a battle would soon develop. Federal leaders knew that the loss of an important city—Washington, Baltimore, or Philadelphia—would be a major victory for the Confederacy and were prepared to fight a major battle to prevent such a loss.

Lee was encouraged by Longstreet to fight purely defensive battles (as they had done at Fredericksburg) in order to inflict severe losses on the Union army, but Lee could not afford to adopt this tactic. He had little room to move about as he had to remain in contact with his extended supply lines in the Shenandoah Valley. His men were able to feed themselves from the rich farms in the area, but an extended stay in a

single area would soon deplete the available food supplies. To construct fortifications and fight a defensive battle in a single location would also seriously deplete the ammunition supply, which was also dependent on the tenuous supply line stretching back through the Shenandoah. The upcoming battle was not of Lee's choosing, but circumstances forced him to fight it. Longstreet had encouraged an attack on the Federal left, placing the Confederate army between the Army of the Potomac and Washington, thereby forcing the Union army to attack. Lee probably felt that the Union army would not be forced to attack, but would play a waiting game as reinforcements arrived daily. Confederate divisions could not move against Baltimore

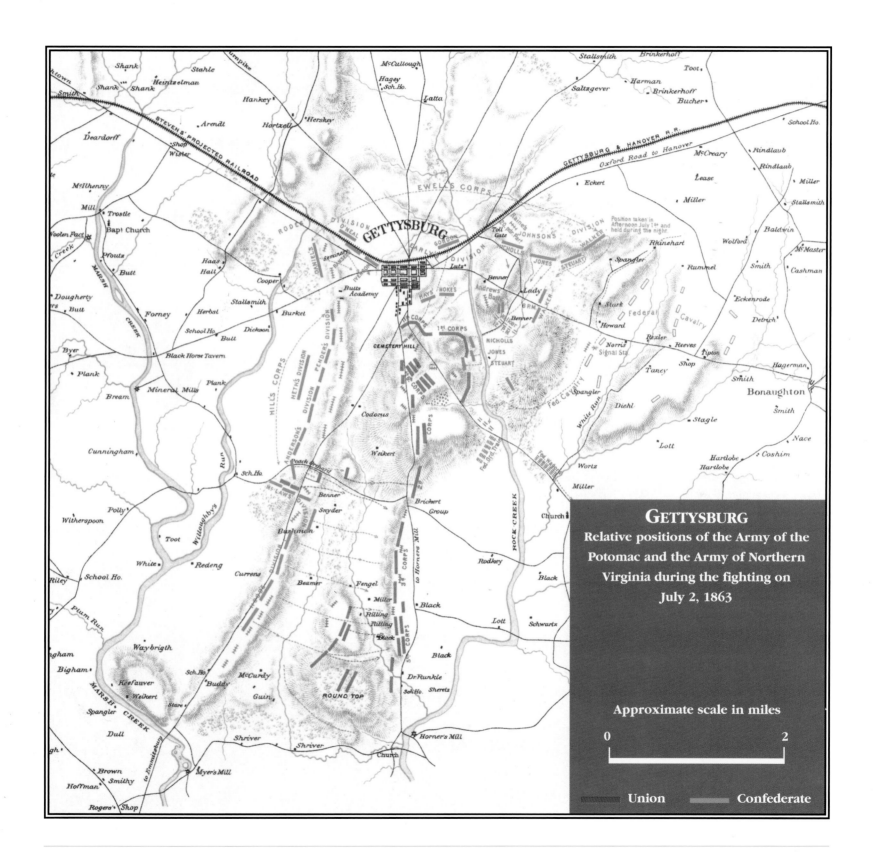

GETTYSBURG

Relative positions of the Army of the Potomac and the Army of Northern Virginia during the fighting on July 2, 1863

Approximate scale in miles

0   2

Union   Confederate

or Washington with an unfought army at their rear, and furthermore the Union army would have no difficulty in feeding its troops, while the Confederate army would be unable to feed itself.

Geography was also against Longstreet's recommendation. Any battle east of Gettysburg would deprive Lee of secure escape routes back through the gaps in the South Mountain range and the prearranged crossings-to-safety in Virginia. Lee felt the immediate and pressing need to fight a battle—a large-scale battle—in Pennsylvania, at a location where a Federal defeat would spell disaster for the Union army, but a Confederate defeat would be manageable for Lee. A movement to the east would put his army in a location where defeat could become a military disaster for the Confederates. Lee had to fight a battle, and Gettysburg was the place where it would be fought.

As the armies drew close to one another, Lee learned from Harrison (a spy, full name unknown) that Hooker had been replaced by Major General George G. Meade on June 28, which was the fifth change of command in the last ten months for the Army of the Potomac. The Confederate army was located northwest of Gettysburg as the Army of the Potomac marched toward them from the southeast. Both armies began to close the gap separating them on June 30 and a severe engagement developed as contact was made in the vicinity of the town.

Meade, a West Point graduate and veteran of the Mexican War, had served competently prior to his recent appointment as a replacement for Hooker and he began to issue orders to his commanders. After learning that Confederates were between Chambersburg and Gettysburg, he ordered three corps of his army to concentrate in the direction of the enemy. John Buford, commanding a Federal cavalry division, entered the excited town just before noon on June 30 and

ABOVE: General George G. Meade, a West Point graduate and veteran of the Mexican War, had received command of a corps after Fredericksburg. Joseph Hooker was overwhelmed by the responsibilities of command and Meade was placed in command of the Army of the Potomac. RIGHT: Confederate James Johnson Pettigrew also charged the Union lines at Gettysburg, but only George Pickett would receive credit for the attack.

found that a Confederate infantry brigade had approached the town and then quickly withdrawn from it. The Confederates, under the command of James Pettigrew, had come to the town to locate shoes, but had withdrawn when the approach of Buford's cavalry was detected. Buford knew the following morning would bring a general engagement in which his troopers would be sorely pressed until the arrival of heavier infantry divisions.

Confederate skirmishers made their initial contact with Buford's pickets at about 5:30 A.M., and severe fighting developed as the Confederates discovered that instead of local militia they were facing the Army of the Potomac. This was a different Union army from the one that had faced the rebel army at Bull Run and in other Virginia battles: poor officers had been replaced as new, experienced officers had risen to command and private soldiers had gained plenty of combat experience. The Federal army had by this time become a large professional army and did not hesitate to engage Lee's upcoming divisions.

Lee gave orders that no general engagement be started on July 1. His army was scattered over unfamiliar terrain within the enemy's territory: Ewell was several hours away to the north and Longstreet's entire corps would need a full day to march in from the west. General Henry Heth (pronounced "Heath") ordered his leading brigades into the town, but they were held up for an hour by Buford's cavalrymen's carbines and horse artillery.

Buford watched the opening rounds of the battle from the top of the Lutheran Seminary building as preparations were made to hold Gettysburg. Additional Union troops—including the Iron Brigade, soldiers who had gained strong reputations for their fighting ability at South Mountain and Antietam—were quickly sent to occupy positions at McPherson's Ridge. As the initial fighting spread, Heth reported that a "heavy force" had been encountered in and around Gettysburg. A short lull developed around noon as reinforcements for both sides began to arrive on the field and soldiers rushed about to occupy various positions.

Men of Ewell's corps, a full division under the command of Major General Robert Rodes, arrived on the field out of the northeast and saw a thinly held line of Federal infantry

TOP: The gatehouse to Evergreen Cemetery on Cemetery Hill. ABOVE: The arrival of General Winfield Scott Hancock on Cemetery Hill during the battle served to rally the retreating soldiers, who rapidly reformed their lines to resist the oncoming Confederates.

in front of them. Sensing an advantage, Rodes ordered an immediate attack. In the rapidly changing situation, additional Federal infantry arrived as Rodes was forming his brigades into attack formations, but at 2 P.M. the Confederate leader ordered an attack. Federal brigades in partially protected positions poured a murderous fire into the Confederate attackers and casualties on both sides were enormous. By the end of the day, Heth had lost fifteen hundred men from his seventy-five-hundred-man division and the Iron Brigade had nearly ceased to exist. Entering the defense of McPherson's Ridge with 1,829 men, the westerners had suffered a staggering 1,153 casualties by the end of the day.

At 3 P.M., the Confederate army began a heavy assault against the Federal defenders in positions north of the town. Ewell's subordinates, Jubal A. Early and Rodes, pressed against the Federal XI Corps from the north and Heth, reinforced by the arrival of William Dorsey Pender's division, attacked I Corps from out of the west. Under this terrible, unrelenting pressure I Corps broke and fled into the town. These men and the soldiers of XI Corps moved through Gettysburg into positions south of the town—Cemetery Hill, Culp's Hill, and Cemetery Ridge—and the two hills at the southern end of the ridge, Little Round Top and Big Round Top.

These were strong positions, but they were long and would require additional reinforcements if the new defensive line was to be held. All available men, including the decimated Iron Brigade, were sent to hold this line as III Corps and XII Corps marched to their aid.

Young Lieutenant Bayard Wilkeson and his small battery, Co. G, 4th U.S. Artillery, fire on the Confederate lines from exposed positions. The nineteen-year-old officer lost his life here.

"It had not been General Lee's intention to deliver a general battle whilst so far from his base, unless attacked, but he now found himself by the mere force of circumstance commited to one."

—General Henry J. Hunt

As the tired, bloodied Federal troops climbed into positions at Cemetery Hill, Lee sent his aide Walter Taylor to Ewell with the request that Ewell continue to push forward, "if practicable," and secure the strategic heights. Ewell, a veteran who had served under Stonewall Jackson—a general who had left no ambiguity in orders to subordinates—was new to command at this level and did not drive forward as the aggressive Jackson might have done in this situation.

It was at this point that Longstreet argued for shifting over to the defensive, into positions between the Army of the Potomac and Washington, and forcing Meade to attack them while they were in strong positions. Lee disagreed with this attempt to change the battle plan in the face of the enemy, and

Severe fighting occurred as defenders met attackers in the fields and hills surrounding Gettysburg. Flags, the most recognizable symbols of the individual combat units, were sought-after trophies, and tremendous fights developed over their possession.

Harvard graduate Colonel Strong Vincent led his brigade to Little Round Top, a strategic position that was soon to receive the attention of the Confederate army. He fell, mortally wounded, while rallying his sorely pressed soldiers; they eventually received reinforcements and were able to hold their positions.

after a delay in the anticipated attack by Ewell, Lee rode to Jackson's successor's headquarters. By the time Lee arrived, the possibility of gaining the advantage had been lost—III Corps and XII Corps had arrived at Cemetery Ridge.

Meade had inspected the new defensive line on the low hills just south of Gettysburg and decided to fight the battle from there.

The morning of July 2 opened with additional troop movements. Longstreet continued to suggest that his battle plan be adopted. Lee declined again and began to issue verbal orders to his corps commanders. Interestingly, Lee prepared no written orders. Also, he seemed to be ill as the battle developed. Some officers reported that Lee was suffering from severe diarrhea, but his illness may have been more severe than these observers thought. The commander had experienced sharp pain in his chest and arms earlier in the year, which may have been symptoms of heart disease—angina—brought on by the stress of battle.

This was less than an excellent day for the Confederate commanders. Longstreet, possibly irritated that Lee had rejected his suggestion as to how to fight the battle, delayed in opening his attack. Regardless of the reason for the delay, Longstreet did not get his corps moving until noon. Unity of command—having one commander in charge during battle—is a basic military principle that was in danger at this point in the battle of Gettysburg. Neither Lee's disappointment at the day's progress nor the pain from his illness were improved by the long-awaited arrival of his missing cavalry commander, Jeb Stuart, to headquarters (Stuart showed up just as Longstreet was ordering his corps into motion).

Lee was visibly angry at Stuart and involuntarily raised his hand as if to strike the tardy cavalry commander. By riding around the entire Federal army (in a raid that may

Little Round Top was the critical point in the Union line. If the Confederate attack had broken through there, the result of the Battle of Gettysburg may have been different.

have been planned to recover some of the prestige he had lost at Brandy Station), Stuart had left Lee without speedy and reliable intelligence in the face of a large army while deep within enemy territory. Lee had been forced to send eight separate couriers riding rapidly through Pennsylvania, in all directions, to deliver the message that a great battle was to be fought at Gettysburg and that Stuart was needed. Fortunately for Stuart, Lee soon put aside his anger and asked for his subordinate's help in winning the battle.

After the delay caused by Lee's preoccupation with the plans of his subordinates, the attack was opened on the second day, after 3 P.M., by Longstreet. One of Longstreet's divisions, commanded by Lafayette McLaws, had expected little or no opposition as he moved into his assigned assault position, but was surprised by a large mass of Federal soldiers in his front and on both flanks. These Union regiments were in positions they should not have occupied.

Curiously, part of the Union army had moved from its assigned position along Cemetery Ridge and left the south flank of the Union defensive line, dangerously weakening it. Meade rode to the commander of the out-of-place troops, Major General Daniel Sickles, but it was too late to pull them back.

The attack had begun and Sickles was dangerously exposed.

At nearly the same time, Confederate General Gouverneur K. Warren discovered a key position, which was undefended, from which artillery, once in position, could fire on the entire Federal line. He ordered the diversion of reserves before Alabama troops could continue their attack from Big Round Top. The war may have been saved for the Union by the aggressive defenders, the 20th Maine commanded by Colonel Joshua Chamberlain, on Little Round Top. Each attack by the Alabama troops was repulsed, but at great cost. The 20th Maine lost 120 men in its defense of Little Round Top.

Sickles' III Corps was forced back from its advanced position with a severe number of casualties, but the main line was secure. Meade was able to shift troops from quiet portions of his line to areas under attack as poorly timed Confederate attacks continued to drive up casualties on both sides. Hill attacked late in the day with minor results and Ewell was unable to get his assault—an

ABOVE: General George Pickett was the commander of the Virginians ordered to attack the Union defenders on Cemetery Ridge. He carried out the order despite the fact that he must have understood the peril his men faced—one of his brigades lost eighty-eight men while waiting to attack. BELOW: Culp's Hill as seen from Cemetery Hill.

attack that should have been timed to coincide with that of Longstreet—launched until around 6 P.M. Ewell's men managed to reach Cemetery Hill, but could not hold their advanced, unsupported positions and were withdrawn. The Army of the Potomac had managed to hold the line against the Army of Northern Virginia.

The third day began with conferences on both sides. Lee was determined to continue with the attack, but Longstreet—as he had throughout the entire battle—had a different opinion. On the Federal side, Meade was unsure of what course to take and made the decision to remain and fight it out on the hills to the south of Gettysburg after a council of his officers recommended that plan.

Ewell would soon be making a diversionary attack at Culp's Hill; the main assault would be made by divisions under the command of Longstreet. Long remembered in history as "Pickett's Charge," the attack against the center of the Union line was composed of three divisions: Pettigrew's, Trimble's, and Pickett's. At 3 P.M., the fifteen

The valiant 1st Maryland Battalion, noted for its extremely brave men, was among the many Confederate forces to be decimated attempting to wrest Culp's Hill from Federal defenders.

thousand Confederate soldiers of these divisions were ordered to march across fourteen hundred yards of open ground toward approximately ten thousand Federal soldiers in protected positions. All of the available Union artillery began to fire into the orderly ranks of Confederate soldiers as they came within range. The effect of the cannon fire was devastating and large numbers of men began to fall. Under fire from artillery as well as volleys from entrenched infantry, the Confederate formations began to entangle as they were forced to the center. General James Kemper tried to get his men moving toward the correct objective, but he himself was severely wounded.

The mob of Confederates in the center of the attack was massed fifteen to thirty deep as General Richard Garnett rode into it to restore order to the assault. Soon after, he was shot from his horse and killed.

The Union defensive line was broken as the Federal artillery position, Cushing's Battery, fired its last double-shotted canister into the attackers. Cushing was killed as General Lewis Armistead placed his hat on the tip of his sword and led his men in a breakthrough. Armistead was mortally wounded as he reached Cushing's guns, but his men pressed onward as nearby Union reserve regiments mounted a counterattack.

The attacker in a case like this is in a difficult position. The losses over the open ground had been tremendous and the Confederate reserves were too far in the rear to be able to exploit the breakthrough. The

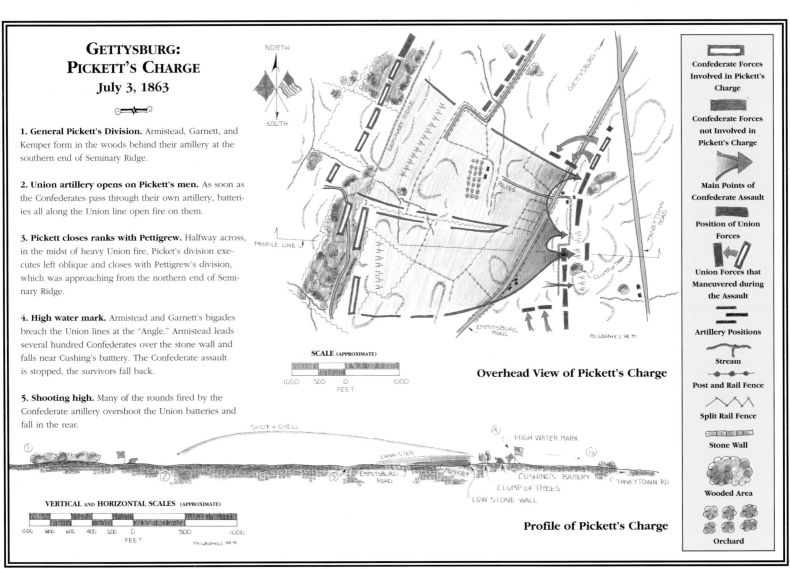

GETTYSBURG: PICKETT'S CHARGE
July 3, 1863

1. General Pickett's Division. Armistead, Garnett, and Kemper form in the woods behind their artillery at the southern end of Seminary Ridge.

2. Union artillery opens on Pickett's men. As soon as the Confederates pass through their own artillery, batteries all along the Union line open fire on them.

3. Pickett closes ranks with Pettigrew. Halfway across, in the midst of heavy Union fire, Picket's division executes left oblique and closes with Pettigrew's division, which was approaching from the northern end of Seminary Ridge.

4. High water mark. Armistead and Garnett's bigades breach the Union lines at the "Angle." Armistead leads several hundred Confederates over the stone wall and falls near Cushing's batttery. The Confederate assault is stopped, the survivors fall back.

5. Shooting high. Many of the rounds fired by the Confederate artillery overshoot the Union batteries and fall in the rear.

SCALE (APPROXIMATE)

1000 500 0 1000
FEET

Overhead View of Pickett's Charge

VERTICAL AND HORIZONTAL SCALES (APPROXIMATE)

1000 800 600 400 200 0 500 1000
FEET

Profile of Pickett's Charge

Confederate Forces Involved in Pickett's Charge

Confederate Forces not Involved in Pickett's Charge

Main Points of Confederate Assault

Position of Union Forces

Union Forces that Maneuvered during the Assault

Artillery Positions

Stream

Post and Rail Fence

Split Rail Fence

Stone Wall

Wooded Area

Orchard

Confederate general Lewis A. Armistead, one of Pickett's brigade commanders, placed his hat upon his sword as he led his men into the Union defenses. He was mortally wounded during the charge and died near his close friend General Winfield Scott Hancock, who was also lying wounded nearby.

surviving attackers who had penetrated into the Union defenses were too few in number to be able to hold their position in the face of the numerous Federal troops who rushed forward to plug the gap in the line. Within minutes, all of the Confederates who had passed into the Union lines were dead, wounded, or taken prisoner. Meanwhile, additional Federal regiments began to converge on the point of the breakthrough.

The attack was over. Large groups of Confederates began to move down the slopes of Cemetery Ridge toward the rear. Pickett had lost nearly half of his soldiers in the attack against the center of the Federal line at Gettysburg. He had lost two generals out of three engaged and the third was severely wounded. Every regimental commander in his division had fallen in the charge. The best of the South's officer corps fell along with very large numbers of soldiers. With the loss of these men, the ability to conduct full-scale offensive operations was also lost to the Confederacy at Gettysburg.

Union artillerymen were instrumental in halting the Confederate Army at Gettysburg. Experienced gunners, well supplied with ammunition, began to decimate Pickett's division as it crossed the broad field at the foot of Cemetery Ridge.

The third day's fighting, however, was not over. General Judson Kilpatrick lived up to his nickname, "Kill Cavalry," by ordering a foolhardy cavalry charge against the right wing of Longstreet. The charge, lead by Brigadier General Elon Farnsworth, resulted in little actual gain, and Farnsworth, who had objected to the plan, was killed in the attack. Stuart was engaged on the other end of the Federal line with his tired troopers

and was repulsed by Federal cavalry as he attempted to attack Meade's northern flank. The battle was coming to an end.

Lee waited for a Federal attack from new positions on Seminary Ridge, but Meade knew the commander of the Confederate army was simply inviting him to attack and avoided the temptation. Moving a company the size of the Union army at Gettysburg from a defensive posture into a counterattack

is extremely difficult and can lead to disaster. Meade had been in command of the Army of the Potomac for only six days and had spent the last three of them fighting one of the most ferocious battles in history. Faced with an opponent who was viewed as a military genius at the time, Meade probably made the correct decision.

A severe storm developed in the afternoon of July 4 and Lee ordered the Army of

Northern Virginia to make its preparations for the return to Virginia. The retreat took days; it was not until July 14 that Lee's army was across the Potomac (his engineers had built a hasty bridge across the river at Falling Waters). With approximately half of the army safely across, the Federal cavalry began its attack. Henry Heth's rear guard, under the command of General Pettigrew, fought tenaciously and broke up the cavalry charge, but Pettigrew himself was mortally wounded. This rear-guard action gave the Army of Northern Virginia the opportunity to escape. The raid into the North had resulted in a terrible loss for the Confederates—one from which they never recovered. As Lee was losing the battle in Pennsylvania, Grant was securing the Mississippi for the Union. The guns fell silent in both places on July 3 and when the dust cleared, it was apparent the rebel states had taken a beating: the Confederacy had been split along the Mississippi while the best army available to the South had been decimated in the North.

Casualties were high on both sides at Gettysburg. Meade lost slightly over twenty-three thousand men, primarily from two of his seven corps—in fact, those two corps ceased to exist at all after the battle. I and III Corps had suffered so many casualties that the survivors were simply incorporated into other commands rather than rebuilt with reinforcements. Confederate losses are estimated differently by various authorities, but they lost at least 20,500 soldiers at Gettysburg. The raw figures, however, don't tell the whole story. Percentagewise, the death count was severe: the Federal army lost 26 percent of its total strength and the Confederates lost approximately 28 percent.

A great deal of controversy remains regarding the conduct of the battle. Lee stated that he would have won the battle if he had had Stonewall Jackson with his army, and this appears to be a reasonable

Federal general Hugh Judson Kilpatrick lived up to his nickname, "Kill Cavalry," by ordering one of his brigades to charge Longstreet's men. The attacking brigade's commander, Elon J. Farnsworth, lost his life in an attack that gained nothing.

> *"One mistake of the Confederacy was in pitting force against force. The only hope we had was to out general the Federals."*
>
> —General James Longstreet

statement: the aggressive Jackson would not have delayed as Ewell had done on the evening of July 1; Jackson's presence would have held the opinions of Longstreet in check; and the unity of command would have been maintained. The outcome of the fighting might have been different. If Lee had won the battle, however, the strategic outcome would have been similar to what is today in the historical record.

Winning the Battle of Gettysburg would have left the Army of Northern Virginia extremely low on ammunition and encumbered it with numerous wounded soldiers requiring transportation and treatment. The Union army would have lost severely and casualties would have been higher than they actually were, but depleted ammunition and

supplies would have been replaced quickly as the army fell back toward major northern cities. Additional troops would have been mobilized to reinforce the Union army.

Winning at Gettysburg would have been a tremendous moral victory for the Confederacy and would have shaken the resolve of the population of the North; then again, the North had suffered severe defeats

ABOVE: Dead Union soldiers found in areas occupied by the Confederates were normally found stripped of both shoes and equipment. Throughout the war Confederate soldiers had little equipment and often went into battle without shoes. RIGHT: Meade and his forces crept forward carefully and crossed the Potomac River two weeks after the Battle of Gettysburg. The slow movement of Meade allowed Lee to escape.

in the past and continued the fight with increased intensity. Anyway, a victory by Lee would have been offset by the simultaneous and decisive victory of Grant at Vicksburg.

The Army of Northern Virginia moved back into Virginia and the remainder of 1863 saw the North and South in what essentially was a stalemate. Meade was slow to go over to the attack, but actions along the Rappahannock River at Bristoe Station, Rappahannock Station, and Kelley's Ford showed that the fighting ability of the Army of Northern Virginia was no longer what it had once been.

When the Army of the Potomac began its next spring offensive, it was under the command of the man who had been winning the war in the west, U.S. Grant. The Army of Northern Virginia would maneuver openly against him only on May 5 and May 6, in the Battle of the Wilderness. The South had lost so much of its former power that Grant was able to continue his advance toward Richmond while Lee's divisions were forced to oppose his attacks from within entrenchments. There would be an entirely different war in 1864.

MONOCACY
Saving Washington

The spring campaign began under new commanders in 1864. Ulysses S. Grant received the message from Secretary of War Stanton naming him commander of all of the Union armies on March 3, 1863. Soon after, Grant convened a hasty meeting with Sherman and they developed a simple plan: Sherman would concentrate his efforts on destroying the Confederate army, under the command of the capable Joseph E. Johnston, in the west. Meanwhile, Grant would focus his efforts on the destruction of the Army of Northern Virginia, which was under the command of Lee.

Grant quickly took advantage of the recent advance in communications technology—the telegraph—to coordinate the moves of all of the Union armies as if they were a single force with a common goal: the destruction of the armies of the Confederacy. Enormous Union forces were now in motion, presenting multiple and simultaneous problems for Lee. On May 4, 1864, the Army of the Potomac crossed the Rapidan to begin the Battle of the Wilderness as other armies began to move in other areas. General Benjamin Butler moved his Army of the James on transports from Fortress Monroe toward Richmond, but was bogged down at Bermuda Hundred when Confederate resistance stiffenened. General Franz Sigel began operations in the Shenandoah Valley on May 2 as generals Crook and Averell began campaigns in southwestern Virginia. Massive operations were in progress against the Confederate army that would continue relentlessly for the next eleven months. If Grant had hoped to get Lee's attention at the opening of the spring campaign, he had clearly succeeded.

Sigel, marching up the Shenandoah Valley (in a southerly direction), presented a threat both to Lee's rear areas and to the vital industrial area of Lynchburg, Virginia. Sigel's march had to be countered, so forces were hastily assembled to oppose him at the small

"[The] situation of Washington was precarious and Wallace moved with considerable promptitude to meet the army at the Monocacy. He could hardly have expected to defeat him,... but he hoped to cripple and delay him."

—General Ulysses S. Grant

town of New Market. Confederate General John Breckinridge hurried forces from southwestern Virginia to block Sigel's advance, but in doing so left a weakened force to oppose Crook and Averell as the Union generals moved to destroy the vital transportation link in the area, the Virginia and Tennessee Railroad.

Confederate defenders met Crook at Cloyd's Mountain as Averell and his cavalry moved to the west to attack Saltville. The battle fought between Crook and Albert Gallatin Jenkins, and later John McCausland, continued for only fifty-two minutes before the Confederates were forced to withdraw, but it was filled with tremendous violence that was matched perhaps only by Antietam. This initial battle of the spring campaign was essentially a draw because Crook and Averell were forced to withdraw into the mountains of West Virginia after destroying the vital bridge over New River.

Sigel continued his march in the Shenandoah even as Crook and Averell were withdrawing. He drew near Breckinridge's waiting regiments, which had been reinforced by cadets from the Virginia Military Institute—young men who were about to experience their first battle. By the end of the day, May 15, Sigel was retracing his steps down the valley. He had been beaten by the

PAGE 85: Resolute Union General Lee Wallace led his men in a crucial defense of Washington, D.C., against Confederate invasion at the Battle of Monocacy. RIGHT: This painting of the heroic charge of the cadets of Virginia's Military Institute is located in the Jackson Memorial Hall. It shows the youthful cadets attacking through heavy fire toward a Federal artillery battery. Their participation in the battle—as Breckinridge's last reserves—closed a gap in the Confederate lines and saved the southern army from probable defeat.

TOP: Virginia's Military Institute cadet Jack Stanard was severely wounded at New Market and died. ABOVE: Cadet F.W. James was also a veteran of New Market.

These five young men from Virginia's Military Institute were already veterans at the time this photograph was taken; they had served at New Market.

hastily assembled troops under Breckinridge. Grant, in no mood to forgive the failure of the political general from Germany, replaced Sigel with General David Hunter. Grant's plan wasn't working well—he had lost forty thousand men since crossing the Rapidan only a few weeks earlier and there were far too few replacements in the depots to satisfy his needs. In addition, the rest of his strategic planning was not going well. The victory at New Market had allowed Breckinridge to send two of his brigades to reinforce Lee just before the Battle of Cold Harbor, where Grant again lost heavily.

LEFT: Federal General Franz Sigel led his small army against John Breckenridge's force on this battlefield. When the guns fell silent, Breckenridge had managed to cripple Sigel's army and temporarily save the Shenandoah Valley for the Confederacy. ABOVE: This antebellum photograph shows John C. Breckenridge when he was Vice President of the United States.

General David Hunter was different from most of the other officers available for command at the time. An aggressive Virginian who had remained with the Union army, he was back on the march in the Shenandoah Valley within a week of assuming Sigel's command. Grant had ordered him to unite with Averell and Crook before moving against and destroying the critical rail junctions at Charlottesville and Lynchburg. He was then to return to his base in the northern part of the valley or reinforce the Army of the Potomac.

As he moved through the rich farm areas toward his goal, Hunter freely retaliated against Confederate partisan raiders and ambushes against his supply line by ordering the burning of every rebel dwelling within five miles of each incident. He was able to defeat the Confederate defenders at the Battle of Piedmont and open the rest of the valley for the safe march of his army to Lynchburg. Confederate Brigadier General John McCausland, the man who had led the attempted breakout at Fort Donelson, was the commander of a small cavalry brigade that remained in front of Hunter, attempting to delay his march. By the time Hunter arrived in front of Lynchburg, the small garrison defending the city had been reinforced by Jubal Early and his infantry corps. Hunter, short of food and ammunition by this time, was forced to retreat into the mountains of West Virginia (and on to supply bases in the Kanawha Valley) in order to avoid the destruction of his command.

The Shenandoah Valley clear of Union forces, Early moved to take full advantage of

Major General David Hunter replaced Sigel after the Union defeat at New Market. Known as "Black Dave" by his own men, this evil-tempered general ordered the destruction of civilian homes in the Shenendoah Valley.

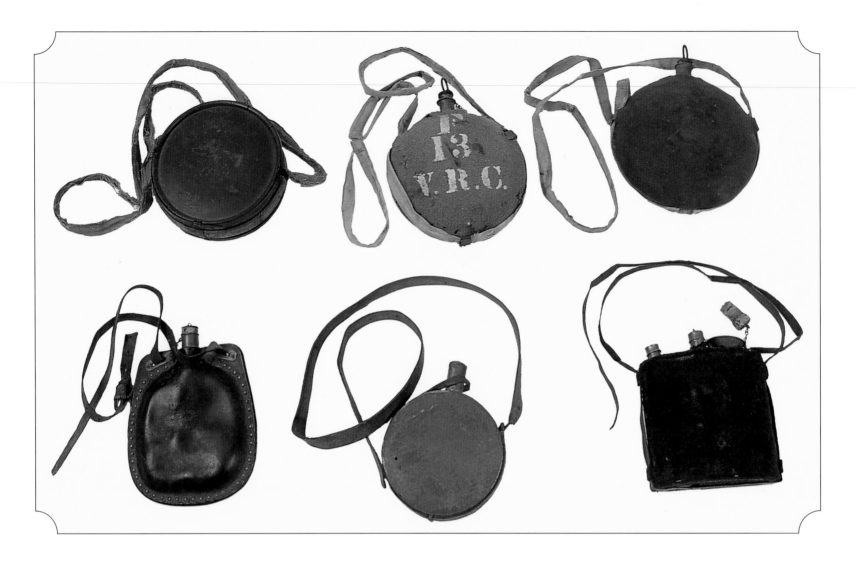

Lacking factories with machinery capable of manufacturing large numbers of military items, the Confederacy was forced to rely on individual craftsmen to manufacture supplies. As a result, individual Confederates could be seen carrying a wide assortment of equipment, as these canteens illustrate.

the situation. He moved quickly, hoping to invade Maryland, force Grant to weaken the forces opposing Lee at Petersburg and Richmond, and attack the defenses of Washington. This was 1864, an election year, and the northern population was beginning to show the strains of the ongoing war. Grant's enormous losses and relatively few gains had contributed greatly to this state of affairs in the North. George McClellan had decided to oppose Lincoln in the fall elections as a peace candidate. An attack against the national capital would clearly serve to weaken the administration.

Early ordered his small army forward. He crossed the Potomac at Shepherdstown on July 5, bypassing the frightened Sigel in barricaded positions on Maryland Heights, and marched quickly on Washington before Grant had time to react. Early decided to ignore Hunter as he moved slowly up the Ohio River and then eastward on the Baltimore and Ohio Railroad toward the South's former base in the Shenandoah Valley. Early may have regarded the attack as a "forlorn hope," a suicide operation, but he continued to advance toward Washington.

Hagerstown, Maryland, would be the first to feel the force of the new invasion; John McCausland captured the town and collected twenty thousand dollars as a ransom (instead of burning it). Early had decided to collect money from northern towns captured to pay for the destructive reprisals that had been undertaken by "Black Dave" Hunter.

McCausland would soon face another veteran of the fighting at Fort Donelson, General Lew Wallace. Currently responsible for the defense of Maryland, Wallace was warned of the upcoming attack by a telegram from John W. Garrett, the president of the Baltimore and Ohio Railroad. Wallace began to gather all available units to defend the open approach to Washington. His was a small army of about twenty-five hundred militia and home guards supplemented by a small cavalry unit, the 8th Illinois Cavalry.

Wallace received his first reinforcements on July 8, when the 10th Vermont arrived from the Army of the Potomac. Grant had finally seen the peril facing Washington and quickly ordered the remainder of VI Corps and two divisions from XIX Corps, then arriving at Fortress Monroe, to Washington.

Early's small army was a real threat, especially because there was the danger that one of his subordinates, Brigadier General Bradley T. Johnson, would be able to free the seventeen thousand Confederate prisoners at Point Lookout prison, effectively doubling the size of Early's army. Johnson was from Frederick, Maryland, and was now involved in the capture of his hometown.

Frederick was to receive the same treatment as had Hagerstown. Once the small city was occupied, Early demanded 200,000 dollars from them to pay for the damage done by Hunter in the Shenandoah Valley. The city fathers of Frederick, however, asked for a delay in making the payment. These shrewd

After forcing David Hunter to retreat westward though West Virginia after Black Dave's attack on Lynchburg had failed, Jubal Early marched north through the Shenendoah Valley. By July 9, 1864, Early's Confederates arrived at the Monocacy River, where they found a smaller Union force under General Lew Wallace waiting for them. A quick victory here would have allowed the small Confederate army to occupy the national capital.

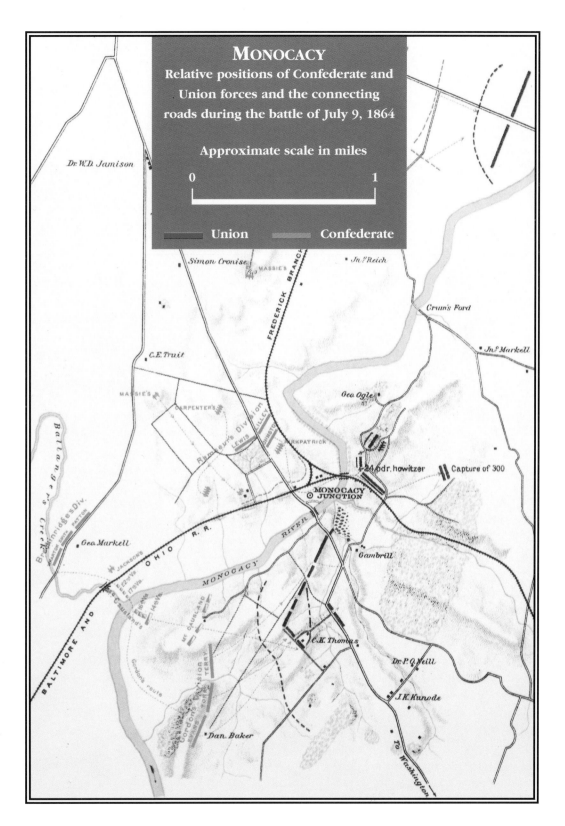

Courageous Confederate General John B. Gordon had suffered severe wounds at Antietam, but continued to fight. In fact, his division did much of the fighting at Monocacy.

Federal General Lew Wallace had distinguished himself at Fort Donelson and although he was not as successful at Shiloh, he saved the Union's capital at Monocacy.

ABOVE: Confederate General Jubal A. Early had voted against leaving the Union during Virginia's Secession Convention, but soon became an unequivocal supporter of the Confederacy. Criticized by many other Confederates at the time, Early managed an excellent campaign in the Shenendoah Valley in 1864. OPPOSITE: Frequently outnumbered and always poorly supplied, the Confederate army fought valiantly for four years and frequently defeated their opponent's larger armies.

businessmen knew that a battle was about to be fought in the vicinity and they were simply waiting to see who would win. Should the Confederates lose, they would save themselves a considerable expense.

Wallace and James B. Ricketts, a division commander in the Union VI Corps, had their men in the best positions available to them outside Frederick by 4 A.M., but the troops began to worry as they saw the huge dust clouds to the west that announced the approach of a large Confederate force.

Early knew that the Union army near Frederick would attempt to dispute his passage, but he was not worried. Bradley Johnson, unaware of the arrival by rail of Rickett's division, had reported that the Federal force was composed of what was essentially raw militia. Crossing the Mono-

cacy River with a substantial portion of his force was Early's immediate concern. He knew his men would have difficulty making the crossing while under fire and that the few bridges were closely held or threatened with immediate destruction. He sent Bradley Johnson north to cut the railroads connecting Frederick to Baltimore and to raid in the vicinity before continuing on to free the Point Lookout prisoners.

Early sent his other cavalry commander, John McCausland, to the south to cut connections with Washington and to seize the railroad bridge over the Monocacy River. McCausland's men located a ford and crossed the Monocacy River, during which they were engaged by men of the 8th Illinois Cavalry. The Federals were driven off, but McCausland was slightly wounded. His cavalrymen

dismounted, leaving their horses with holders, and continued with the attack—reduced in strength by one hundred men. Seven hundred of McCausland's dismounted troopers were moving against a fence that they mistakenly supposed was being held by local militia. Instead, seasoned veterans from the Army of the Potomac were concealed and waiting.

The horse holders remained in the rear as McCausland's dismounted men began their advance through the waist-high corn toward a force three times their size behind the

ABOVE: This is a Federal cavalry bugler uniform jacket (left) and an artillery bugler uniform jacket (right). Union cavalry units were poorly used during the early parts of the war and jokes such as "Have you ever seen a dead cavalryman?" were often heard. This attitude, however, changed as new, aggressive cavalry commanders rose in the Union ranks. By the end of the war, Federal cavalrymen operated as highly mobile mounted infantrymen and they made a difference on many battlefields. RIGHT: The 8th Illinois Cavalry engaged McCausland's troopers at Monocacy in a dismounted skirmish. BELOW: Spencer carbine bullets of the type used by Union cavalry.

boundary fence. When the Confederates came into range, the Federal soldiers rose and fired a disciplined volley into the surprised cavalrymen. When the smoke cleared from the cornfield, it appeared to be empty. Survivors of the murderous volley were slipping to the rear, but many were dead or wounded. McCausland made a personal reconnaissance of the Federal positions and gathered his men for a second attempt that was more successful. Only a strong leader in charge of seasoned, disciplined troops would have been able to get his men to attack a second time. Unable to hold the exposed positions they captured, McCausland's cavalrymen again withdrew. Shortly afterward Major General John Gordon crossed the river with his infantry division.

The work of the cavalry was the key to the opening of the battle. Early, though long a critic of the cavalry, wrote that "Gordon moved across the Monocacy on the enemy's flank by a route that had been opened by McCausland's brigade of cavalry in a very gallant manner." McCausland's cavalrymen moved off to the south to block a retreat toward Washington by Wallace or the arrival of Union reinforcements.

Buglers, who were often adolescents, used bugles such as this one to signal commands to widely separated cavalrymen.

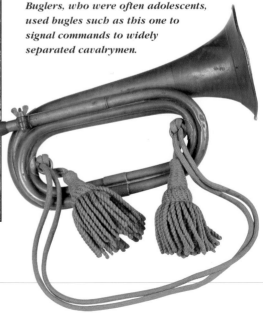

Buglers were normally found with the cavalry commanders' staff and many were killed or wounded while serving their country.

Gordon's division was in attack position by 3 P.M. Lew Wallace reassessed the situation. He wanted to evacuate from overextended positions that could be easily attacked on its flank and rolled up, but he could not retreat in the face of an imminent attack by Gordon. They had to remain and fight. Gordon, a veteran of much of the combat up to this point in the war, was eager to accommodate them.

Gordon's soldiers advanced in the face of very heavy fire, losing men every few feet, across a field that was filled with shocks of freshly cut wheat, obstacles that forced them to break their formations. Gordon's attack began to bog down despite covering fire from several guns across the Monocacy under the command of Major William McLaughlin (in whose unit one of the author's ancestors served). These guns were fired at Federal sharpshooters concealed in a house on the battlefield. Reinforcements were rushed to aid Gordon; General Ricketts hurriedly moved his Union soldiers to shore up the threatened line, but this was precisely what the Confederate commanders wanted him to do. The thinned right side of the Federal line could no longer be anchored against the obstacle of the Monocacy River, opening it to a Confederate flank attack. Gordon quickly sent a Virginia brigade against the weakened right side of the Federal line of defense and forced the veterans to pull back, but not before the Federal soldiers inflicted severe casualties on the attacking Virginians. Ricketts was forced to withdraw while under fire, but he and his VI Corps veterans were able to move to the rear without the retreat becoming a retreat. The firing slowed and halted; it was too late in the day for Early to continue the attack.

Lew Wallace, who later wrote *Ben Hur*, had bought twenty-four hours for the defenders of Washington to prepare themselves while they waited for reinforcements to

Exhausted, poorly supplied, and hungry, Confederate soldiers were capable of making tremendous sacrifices in the face of overwhelming numbers of Union soldiers. Regardless of the Confederates' reasons for fighting, the mystique of their heroism lives on to this day.

"If Early had been but one day earlier, he might have entered the capital before the arrival of the reinforcements I had sent."

—*General Ulysses S. Grant*

arrive. The Battle of Monocacy had cost the Union 1,294 casualties, but the capital was saved. Early lost approximately seven hundred men—who could not be replaced—but continued to advance toward his target.

The Confederates moved down the dusty, hot roads toward Washington. They passed through Silver Spring, and by noon on July 11, Jubal Early was surveying Fort Stevens and planning his attack. His soldiers were exhausted—even the veteran, disciplined troops were worn out after the hot march. They were too tired to assault the Federal defensive line, which was held by hastily organized groups of walking wounded, convalescents, and untrained government clerks. Reinforcements from the VI and XIX Corps were en route, however.

The first men from VI Corps reached the trenches surrounding the capital in the early afternoon of July 11, and Jubal Early had lost his opportunity to win the war for the Confederacy. Severe skirmishing continued as the small Confederate army fought with the Federal reinforcements through July 12, but there would be no general attack. Early had ordered the division commanders to be ready to move in the night and had recalled Bradley Johnson from the raid against Point Lookout.

President Lincoln came out to Fort Stevens to watch the battle and actually came under hostile fire, but there was no large-scale attack on July 12. Early was going back to the relative safety of the Shenandoah Valley before the assembling Federal armies at his rear were able to box his small army up and destroy it. He crossed the Potomac at White's Ford and rested at Leesburg, Virginia, before continuing his march.

Early continued to hold the Shenandoah Valley into the late summer and sent John McCausland north into Pennsylvania in late July. Ordered to capture Chambersburg and collect a ransom or burn the small city, McCausland set torches to the buildings when the townspeople refused (or were unable) to comply. This raid revealed the continuing threat to Washington presented by Confederates in the Shenandoah; Grant ordered substantial forces to move there and destroy Early and his army. Defeated at Winchester on September 19, Early was forced up the valley, but was able to fight a successful battle against enormous odds at Cedar Creek on October 19. His small force was overwhelmed later in the day, ending Confederate dominance in this critical area of Virginia.

The Battle of Monocacy was small when compared to Gettysburg and many of the transition battles of the Civil War. It was, however, possibly the most crucial battle of the war. If Lew Wallace had been unable or unwilling to fight this delaying action, Early would have been attacking the defenses of Washington one day before any substantial reinforcements from VI and XIX Corps could have arrived. The Confederates would have been unable to hold the national capital, but the crucial loss to Early in mid-July would have doomed the Republican administration and Abraham Lincoln in the November elections. George McClellan, the peace candidate, may have been elected, and as president would have witnessed an entirely different outcome to the Civil War.

Lew Wallace and his small Union force were able to delay Early's Confederates for a full day, allowing reinforcements from Grant's army at Petersburg to enter Washington, D.C. Wallace's men saved the nation's capital from occupation and probably saved Lincoln's political career. Years later, veterans of the 15th New Jersey Infantry erected this monument on Monocacy battlefield to commemorate their deeds of 1864.

PEACHTREE CREEK
Breaking Connecting Links

Two rather ordinary looking soldiers met in a Cincinnati hotel room during March 1864; only the stars on their shoulder straps gave a hint as to the importance of their meeting. These two men were Ulysses S. Grant, commander of all of the armies of the United States, and his chief lieutenant, William T. Sherman, now the commander of Union forces in the west, Grant's previous position. The two Ohio-born officers had been friends for much of the war and remained close at this time. Sherman later described the reason for the relationship: "He stood by me when I was crazy and I stood by him when he was drunk; and now we stand by each other always."

The two West Point graduates had planned to press their adversaries relentlessly; the key operations would be in northern Virginia and in northern Georgia. Grant would remain in the field with the Army of the Potomac and engage Robert E. Lee and his Army of Northern Virginia until it was defeated in battle. Sherman was charged with the task of engaging and destroying the other large Confederate formation, the Army of Tennessee under Lee's classmate, Joseph E. Johnston. These Confederate commanders were well-trained, educated and experienced in the arts of war, and their armies were defending their home territories. The tasks the two Union commanders set themselves were by no means easy to accomplish; and to succeed, the attacks had to be coordinated and simultaneous. Sherman told his quartermaster: "I'm going to move on Joe Johnston the day Grant telegraphs me he is going to hit Bobby Lee."

Grant's letter of instruction to Sherman was simple: "You I propose to move against Johnston's army, to break it up and get into the interior of the enemy's country as far as you can, inflicting all the damage you can upon their war resources." Sherman was given no specific target, but Atlanta was an obvious first goal.

> "[The] plan, promptly adopted, was simple and comprehensive: To break and keep broken the connecting links of the enemy's opposing armies, beat them one by one, and unite for a final consumption. Sherman's part was plain."
>
> —General Oliver Howard

Siege of Atlanta
Relative positions of Confederate and Union forces during the siege of July 19–August 26, 1864

Approximate scale in miles

0   1

Union   Confederate

William Tecumseh Sherman, a trusted subordinate of Grant, was sent to destroy Joseph E. Johnston's Confederate army.

Sad, sleepy-eyed John Bull Hood received his first army command after Braxton Bragg recommended to President Jefferson Davis that Johnston be replaced.

Atlanta had become a vital rail hub, arsenal, and manufacturing center that supported the Confederate war effort. In importance, it was second only to Richmond and its industries turned out war supplies of every description. The railroads from the city carried grain and other forms of food from farms throughout the region and delivered it to Confederate armies in the field.

As Sherman made his preparations to move, Joseph Johnston was also readying his men for the inevitable spring offensive from the Union army. He was prepared for the job in front of him. He had once led the Army of Northern Virginia, but had suffered severe wounds at the Battle of Fair Oaks in 1862, and had been replaced by Lee. This experienced commander brought order and a high state of morale to the Army of Tennessee, the force that had been experiencing extremely high rates of desertion since the defeat under Braxton Bragg at Lookout Mountain and Missionary Ridge that had cost the Confederacy Chattanooga.

Johnston gave a general amnesty to soldiers who freely rejoined their units and developed a system of furloughs to permit his men to visit their families during the winter. But he was also tough: many deserters stood at the foot of their graves while facing

a firing squad. He organized his command into two corps, one under William Hardee, a veteran soldier who had participated in most of the fighting in the west. The other corps went to John B. Hood, a veteran of the Army of Northern Virginia. The Army of Tennessee was preparing for renewed war under tested commanders, one of whom (Johnston) they came to love with a reverence that approached the regard Lee's men held for him. Johnston took care of his men and they trusted him as their commander.

While Johnston may have won the full respect of his officers and men, he was far less popular in Richmond. Jefferson Davis harbored an extreme dislike—which approached distrust—for the general. A dispute developed between the two West Point graduates early in the war during which Johnston's

seniority had been invoked. Johnston had apparently antagonized Davis by not explaining his exact reasons for moving to Richmond following the victory at Bull Run. John Bell Hood entered into this political intrigue by sending a series of secret reports to Davis that painted a picture that differed from the one reported by Johnston. Hood may have been so disabled that he had to be strapped to his saddle, but he was ambitious and managed to undermine the slight amount of confidence Davis had in General Joe Johnston.

Johnston continued to prepare for the invasion he knew would come. He fortified positions on Rocky Face Ridge, a large ridge located a few miles west of Dalton, Georgia, and began the first campaign of the Confederacy with a strategy that matched the resources available. Johnston's strategy was one of defensive maneuver, which permitted his forces to move from one strong defensive position to another while inviting Sherman to make expensive frontal attacks. This campaign was one of the best-managed operations of the entire Civil War.

Sherman moved against Johnston on May 4, 1864 (the same day Grant crossed the Rapidan to begin the Battle of the Wilderness). Fighting occurred each day as Sherman forced his way south, repeatedly encountering strong positions set in his path. Sherman's armies—there were three under his command—would outflank Johnston. Johnston, in turn, would move back to prepared positions and wait for the arrival of the Union army—again.

Hood decided to open an attack of his own on June 22 near a large plantation, Kolb's farm, without the permission of Johnston. Unfortunately for Hood and his men, his preparations for the general assault had been revealed by prisoners and confirmed by skirmishers who were close enough to hear Hood's preparations. The attack struck a Federal force that outnumbered the Confederates. In addition, the Union defenders were ensconced in the relative safety of breastworks constructed just prior to the attack. Cannons fired into the attacking lines with canister and many of Hood's men fell. The Confederates withdrew, re-formed, and renewed their costly attack, then withdrew again. It remains a mystery why Hood ordered the unauthorized attack, but the results are clear: Hood lost nearly one thousand men and failed to report the full results of the error to Johnston.

This slow-paced campaign began to have an effect on the morale of Sherman's command. On June 27, slowed by muddy roads, Sherman decided to attack Johnston in a frontal assault at Kennesaw Mountain, where the Confederates waited in prepared

"I was informed... Thomas was building bridges across Peach Tree Creek.... I percieved at once that the Federal commander had committed a severe blunder in separating his Corps."

—General John B. Hood

positions. The Confederate army was able to fight a defensive battle, evacuate their entrenchments, and move into a new and elaborate line that had been prepared for them by slaves (by contrast, the Union soldiers had to dig their own trenches).

Sherman's plan was simple and was based on the assumption that Johnston had strengthened his vulnerable flanks at the expense of the center. Sherman's entire army would press the whole Confederate line, thereby occupying them while two assault columns would strike into the center of the defensive works. The Union army had not fully absorbed the lesson of Cold Harbor in the east: regiments attacking troops of near-equal strength in defensive positions suffer enormous casualties and gain little. Sherman

lost nearly three thousand men at Kennesaw Mountain while Johnston lost a quarter of that number. Sherman had seen war and knew that men must die while fighting it and planned another attack. Meanwhile, one of his commanders, John Schofield, managed to outflank the Kennesaw Mountain positions that had been causing the Union forces so much trouble.

Anticipating Sherman's move, Johnston moved to another defensive line near the railroad at Smyrna. He then moved again, to the north bank of the Chattahoochee River, with the river at his rear—a location from which no sane man would fight. Sherman saw the slave-built fortifications and pronounced them "one of the strongest pieces of field fortifications I ever saw," but he could also see Atlanta in the distance.

He sent John Schofield upstream, where lightly armed Confederates were scattered, without the loss of a Federal soldier. By midnight, Schofield had built two pontoon bridges and ordered two divisions across into the expanding bridgehead.

Flanked again, Johnston was compelled to abandon his strong positions on the Chattahoochee River and march to new positions on a ridge behind Peachtree Creek. This new defensive line was only five miles from Atlanta. It was at this point that political influence began to have an impact on the operation. Braxton Bragg, Johnston's predecessor, arrived in Atlanta on July 13 on an "unofficial" visit. Bragg was now Jefferson Davis' military advisor. He met with Hood before he went to see Johnston; the disabled

OPPOSITE: Sherman decided on June 27, 1864, to attack General Joseph E. Johnston's prepared positions on Kennesaw Mountain. Sherman lost three thousand men in this conflict and Johnston was able to withdraw to a new line.

PEACHTREE CREEK

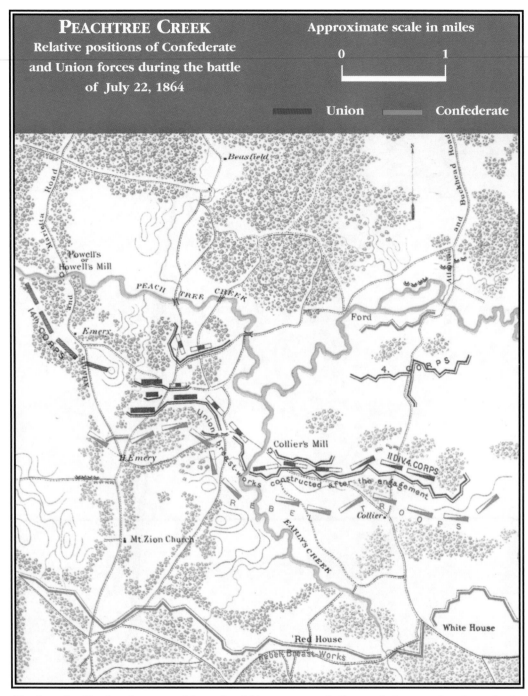

The day after Hood took command, he ordered his men to attack Sherman's forces at Peachtree Creek. Although the poorly executed and uncoordinated attacks caught the Union army off guard, the Confederates lost twice the number of casualties as the Federals—men the southern army could not afford to lose.

but ambitious general bent Bragg's ear, undermining Johnston's postition as commander of the Army of Tennessee and promoting himself.

Johnston had about as much respect for Braxton Bragg as he had for Davis, and said of the Confederate president: "He tried to do what God failed to do. He tried to make a soldier of Braxton Bragg...." The combination of Bragg, Davis, and the reports of Hood were too much for Johnston to defend against and Davis relieved him of command. The combative, and possibly reckless, Hood assumed his command.

John Bell Hood is an interesting historical figure at this point in the Civil War. Always brave and reckless, he had been severely disabled by wounds; in fact, he had lost a leg before being ordered to northern Georgia. Hood was reported to be in extreme pain from his war wounds and may have been taking large amounts of an opiate called laudanum to relieve his discomfort. It is altogether possible that the painkiller interfered with his judgment. Curiously, he had also developed a new interest in religion as he entered into this series of battles and asked Leonidas Polk, a West Point graduate who was an Episcopal bishop of Louisiana and a Confederate general, to baptize him. A case could be made that Hood was preparing for his eventual death, and some historians have felt that his tactics during the remainder of the Civil War hinted tantalizingly of intentions of suicide.

Hood was known to be a bold and aggressive fighter, but he had commanded only smaller units in the past. He was entirely inexperienced at this level of command. Sherman was warned by Hood's West Point roommate, John Schofield, that Hood could be expected to "...hit you like Hell..." but Sherman was pleased with the change of command in the Confederate headquarters. He had been dealing with the delaying tactics of Johnston for over three months and

Benjamin Harrison, a future president of the United States, gained distinction by closing a dangerous gap in the Union line during the Battle of Peachtree Creek.

General Grenville Dodge, a professional railroad engineer before the war, would survive the war and go on to work for the Union Pacific railroad, helping the U.P. to connect the east and west coasts.

General George H. Thomas, a Virginian who remained in the Federal army, had proven his ability in Tennessee. He gained the nickname "Rock of Chickamauga" in the Battle of Chickamauga by saving the Union from total defeat.

was happily anticipating open combat with the Confederate army.

On July 19, the day after Hood took command, the Confederate commander noticed a flaw in the arrangement of the Federal divisions facing him and made some hasty plans. A gap had developed in the alignment of the armies of Schofield and Thomas as they marched into the swampy ground near Peachtree Creek; Hood made plans to attack. His plan was good but the execution was flawed.

Peachtree Creek was Hood's first battle as an independent commander and delays were encountered as the Confederate army moved into positions from which they would attack. The Confederate columns were late and the attack began at 4 P.M. The

attacks were uncoordinated, but the Confederates managed to catch the Federal army off guard as it prepared to stop for the night. Sherman's army, used to doing the attacking against the Confederates in their breastworks, were completely unprepared for the violent attack. Confederate commander William Bate's division charged directly toward a bridge over the creek; once across, he would be in a position to block a Federal retreat.

George Thomas, the Union army commander at that location, was able to move an artillery battery into position to defend the bridge and break up the Confederate attack. Other of his divisions faced the prospect of being flanked and overwhelmed when a counterattack lead by Colonel Benjamin

Harrison, a future U.S. president, closed a break in the Federal defensive line and consolidated the defenders' positions as Hardee, the Confederate corps commander, prepared to order in his reserves.

The reserve division was one of the best in the Confederate army and was under the command of an excellent commander, Patrick Cleburne. Cleburne's men were to be sent in against Thomas' divisions in a last effort to win the battle before dark, but the orders were changed at the last moment.

While Thomas' Army of the Cumberland was under this severe attack, another of Sherman's units, the Army of the Tennessee under Major General James McPherson, had moved within artillery range of Atlanta and fired its first rounds, threatening the

Confederate troops move forward as they march to attack Logan's corps near Atlanta.

off guard. He had been warned of Hood's movements, but the Union commander thought that they were the initial evacuation of Atlanta and was not alarmed. Fortunately for the Union commander, McPherson had ordered one of his corps commanders, Grenville Dodge, to move to positions on the Federal left flank and Dodge's XVI Corps was in position as Hardee's divisions struck.

To the left of this fighting, Cleburne's division located a gap in the Federal defensive line and nearly broke into the rear of the entire Union line before being forced back in severe combat. As the ferocity of Hardee's attack diminished, Hood finally ordered a supporting attack, but it was too late to make any difference in the outcome of the day's fighting. The Federal army lost heavily, however. General McPherson, a young West Point graduate and commander of the Army of the Tennessee, was killed as

Confederate cavalry defending the Georgia Railroad. Cleburne was diverted to support the cavalry, and the battle of Peachtree Creek was over. Hood had lost approximately three thousand men, twice the number of casualties suffered by the Union army, and the attack had gained nothing for the defenders of Atlanta. The impetuous new commander had failed in his initial attack in the open.

Hood faced the dilemma of the defender: he had to attempt to protect all approaches to Atlanta while defending each important target. Sherman had a great advantage and could pick and choose among weaker targets, attacking on his own schedule (as he had done with Johnston). Sherman underestimated the aggressive Hood, however, and

was soon facing a renewed assault by the tired Confederates.

Hood had to contend with the possibility that McPherson would continue his march to the east of Atlanta, bypass the Confederate positions, and march into the city to capture it. Hood briefed his commanders on a plan that would get his troops into the rear of the Army of the Tennessee by attacking around McPherson's southern flank. The orders to begin a long, fifteen-mile march in the dark were issued to Hardee's divisions on July 21, but delays and tired men held up their arrival until noon on July 22. Hardee had made it into a position in McPherson's rear and opened the attack just after noon. Confederate divisions smashed into Federal defenders in an attack that caught Sherman

Major General James B. McPherson was the only Union army commander ever to die in battle.

he rode from Dodge's position to threatened units just to the west. He was shot by skirmishers from Cleburne's division as he tried to avoid capture, becoming the only commander of a Federal army to die in the war.

The battle continued through the remainder of the day, but the combative Hood's repeated attacks cost him nearly eight thousand men, more than twice his losses at Peachtree Creek only two days earlier. Sherman had also lost heavily: 3,722 men died, including General McPherson, for whom Sherman grieved.

By July 28, 1864, the Confederates held only a single railroad supply line into the city, the Macon and Western Railroad. Sherman planned to disrupt the railroad twenty miles south of Atlanta and moved two columns in a converging movement against it.

Hood moved four divisions to stop Sherman and approached Oliver O. Howard,

McPherson's replacement, near a small church called Ezra Church. Howard chose good defensive positions and prepared for an attack. He was cautious and suspected that Hood, always a fighter, would be sending his divisions against him.

Howard's premonition had been right. Hood's men had been lured out of their fortifications a third time in only a few days. Stephen Lee, as aggressive as Hood, drove against the Federal field fortifications again

LEFT: Having earlier fought in the Army of the Potomac, General Oliver O. Howard fought in the Atlanta campaign and survived to become the founder of Howard University in Washington, D.C. BELOW: Union artillery positions surrounded Atlanta.

and again. By 5 P.M., the battle slowed to a halt and the Confederates had again lost heavily. About five thousand Confederates died in this engagement. (Overall, Hood had lost nearly one third of his men in the ten days he had been in command). Federal units, in the relative safety of their hastily constructed breastworks, lost only about six hundred men.

The Union army moved closer to Atlanta and began a heavy cannonade: five thousand shells struck the interior of the city. The citizens tried to survive the shelling by sheltering in dugout "bombproofs," but several died in the first bombardment. Sherman hoped to develop a new tactic to draw the rest of Hood's army out into the open where it could be destroyed, but the fighting settled down into a stalemate.

The doomed city still needed supplies, which had to be delivered over the railroad. Attacks against the railroads had brought Hood out before, so Sherman selected the Macon and Western Railroad as the next target and ordered his entire army to move to Jonesboro. Confederate scouts reported the departure of the Federal army from its positions and Hood thought this was a Union retreat, a grave miscalculation on his part.

Once again, the defenders of Atlanta were ordered to rush against the prepared defenses of the Union army. The Federal soldiers had all the time they needed to dig rifle pits and build fortifications as the Confederate army began to mass at Jonesboro on September 1.

RIGHT, TOP: General William T. Sherman pressed his armies forward in Georgia until Atlanta was besieged. Sherman, a practitioner of modern warfare, struck economic targets that were crucial to his enemy's ability to fight. RIGHT: The railroads that allowed supplies and produce to be shipped to the Confederate army were destroyed. Rails were heated and then bent, rendering the tracks useless.

Hood's ordnance train was destroyed by fire; the flames destroyed a factory near Atlanta.

The fighting was severe and the Confederates suffered many casualties. They were learning the lesson Johnston had taught to Sherman early in the campaign. Union divisions behind the fortifications lost 179 men while the attackers lost 1,725—men Hood could not afford to lose. Worse still, Hardee had to face alone the onslaught of the Federal army. A slow attack using just a single corps cost Sherman thirteen hundred men and an opportunity to trap Hardee's Confederate corps. Hardee's men began to slip away to the south of Atlanta at midnight and the rest of the defenders were also on the march. The city was being evacuated; Sherman had won.

Sherman sent a telegram to Lincoln on September 3, announcing the capture of the city, nearly ensuring the reelection of Lincoln in November. He had captured a vital rail and industrial center that supplied the Confederacy, but he had not been able to destroy Johnston's Confederate army as Grant had instructed him to do.

On November 30, 1864, the volatile Confederate General John B. Hood led the depleted Army of Tennessee against Union defenders commanded by Major General John Schofield in the city of Franklin, Tennessee. The Rebels were repulsed largely thanks to the bravery of Colonel Emerson Opdycke (wielding his spent pistol as a club) and the six regiments under his command.

PEACHTREE CREEK

Atlanta's Peachtree Street was severely damaged during the Federal seige. An important city to the Confederacy because it was a center for industry and a transportation hub, Atlanta was the initial goal of General Sherman's army.

Johnston had shown his skill as a commander when faced with one of the most aggressive of the Union's generals. His strategy had been one of trading space for time while keeping his defenders well concentrated. It was probably the best approach for the Confederacy at this stage of the war. Their manpower and general resources could not sustain a maneuver campaign of attack such as that waged by Hood in the final days of the campaign. Hood had lost more men in ten days than Johnston had lost in the previous 118 days while delaying Sherman's approach toward Atlanta.

The sound of exploding ammunition and locomotives could be heard by the Federal troops at Jonesboro as the Confederate reserve ammunition was destroyed. Hood's army was so weak that Sherman could now virtually ignore it and proceed with his original plan. He sent thirty thousand men back into Tennessee to defend the area against Hood's depleted Confederate divisions while he marched out of Atlanta with over sixty thousand men toward the Atlantic Ocean.

Hood attacked at Franklin, Tennessee, in a hopeless frontal assault against Federal entrenchments that cost the Confederacy the services of Patrick Cleburne, twelve other general officers, and eight thousand men. Hood was attacked at Nashville in a flawlessly planned battle orchestrated by George Thomas. The overextended Confederate line, concave to the enemy's front and denied the coveted interior lines, was severely defeated; in fact, the force was eliminated from the Civil War and the impetuous Hood was relieved from command.

Sherman moved from Atlanta after burning public buildings, destroying all of the railroads in the immediate vicinity, and forcing the city's population to evacuate. He did this to avoid the necessity of leaving a large garrison to control the city, which would reduce his available manpower. He then followed the example of Grant in the Vicksburg campaign by breaking away from his supply lines. He marched forward on a sixty-mile front with emergency rations for twenty days and intentions of living off the country until the Union army reached the seacoast, where they could be resupplied by the navy.

The strategy was simple: wage economic war on a scale similar to that being waged in the Shenandoah Valley by Sheridan, who was marching his divisions toward the Virginia theater of operations to reinforce Grant and eliminate Lee's Army of Northern Virginia. Sherman arrived at Savannah, Georgia, on December 21 and offered the city to the nation as a Christmas present. He continued his destructive march, carrying the destruction and terror of the war directly to the Confederate population.

The key point in the complex Atlanta campaign, however, had been the battle of Peachtree Creek. The decision to replace Joseph Johnston, a man who had designed an excellent strategy that efficiently used the meager resources available, with John Bell Hood, a combative, aggressive commander who had never had an independent command, had proven to be decisive.

Engaging the Union army in the open was suicidal, especially for Hood, who was untried at senior command and experienced only in aggressively executing the plans of others. His army, through poorly timed and often uncoordinated attacks, suffered heavy casualties. Davis' dislike of Johnston, combined with Hood's behind-the-scenes maneuvering, had cost the South dearly at Atlanta. And Hood continued to lose from that point onward in the campaign.

The war was entering the final year.

chapter 8

FIVE FORKS
Carrying Everything Before Them

The last year of the Civil War began and ended in much the same way. Grant was in front of Lee at Petersburg, defending Richmond, the Confederate capital, and Sherman was in Georgia moving to unite his forces with Grant. When Grant had crossed the Rapidan in May, both he and Lee were at the height of their military careers. Grant had won many major victories in the west and Lee had become a legend in the various campaigns in the eastern theater.

After crossing the Rapidan, Grant chose to move along Lee's right flank. Movement along this route allowed him to plan to resupply his forces along Virginia's tidewater rivers and the Chesapeake Bay rather than depend on an enormous wagon train, which would be complicated by the need to care for thousands of horses and mules. Understandably, Grant wanted to concentrate his forces and deploy them effectively in battle rather than use many of them to care for the supply animals.

The two opposing generals met on May 5 in the Battle of the Wilderness, in the same locale where Hooker had lost badly the year before. The fighting consisted of attack and counterattack in tangled brush that caught fire, killing many of the wounded (as had happened at Fort Donelson two years earlier). Lee attacked again on May 6, but neither side was able to gain a clear advantage.

It was at this point in Grant's career that he would show that he was different from all of the commanders of the Army of the Potomac who had served before him. They had always returned to the relative safety of the north side of the Rappahannock after an encounter with Lee, but Grant issued different orders. Ignoring his losses, and relying on his numerical superiority, Grant continued to march southward in an attempt to get between Lee and Richmond. Both armies raced for the vital crossroads at Spotsylvania, but Lee arrived first and began to construct fortifications, defenses behind which his men

of Gaines' Mill, where Grant had attacked Lee's entrenched center with his infantry and suffered tremendous losses. Grant later admitted his error in ordering the costly attack at Cold Harbor: "Cold Harbor, I think, is the only battle I ever fought that I would not fight over again under the circumstances." The Battle of Cold Harbor completed a month of heavy fighting that cost the Federal army fifty-five thousand casualties and Lee thirty-two thousand. Grant continued to press his army to the south.

Once the Union army arrived at the James River, Grant's engineers built a twenty-one-hundred-foot pontoon bridge—the longest in history up to that time—and his entire army crossed to the south bank. Following his initial strategy, on June 18 Grant established a supply base, complete with a railroad, at City Point. He then began siege operations against the city of Petersburg, below Richmond, and continued to invest until the following year. Grant was able to view the war as a continuous battle as he clung closely and tenaciously to Lee's army. The war in Virginia had evolved into trench warfare, where siege guns and mortars were used extensively. The firepower and destructive potential of the modern, rifled weapons available to both sides had practically eliminated infantry charges as a battle tactic. Losses were simply too common for either side to attempt this approach. Cold Harbor had taught the commanders well.

Grant continued to move to cross Lee's southern flank and the Confederate army matched each of the Federal movements with new trenches and fortifications. Curiously, these two masters of mobile warfare, Lee and Grant, were reduced to maneuvering their fortifications. Lee had been drawn into a situation that he feared most, a protracted siege in the front of the Confederate capital, Richmond. Earlier in the year Lee had astutely observed to Jubal Early, "We must destroy

would fight for the remainder of the Civil War. The Battle of Gettysburg had bled the Confederate officer corps and army to the point that it could no longer maneuver in the open against strong forces like Grant's.

The field fortifications proved strong: the Army of the Potomac attacked them for four days, beginning on May 9, but the Confederates beat back each assault. On two separate occasions, Grant's army was able to break through and each time was unable to exploit the situation. Grant, however, had made a fateful decision at Spotsylvania and wrote to General Halleck that he intended to "fight it out on this line if it takes all summer." The losses he had suffered and his inability to draw Lee's army into the open convinced Grant that the best strategy lay in moving his army to the south in an attempt to envelop Lee's right flank. This process of slipping south continued for the Federal army while Lee, with smaller numbers, skillfully moved to remain between the invading Federal army and Richmond.

By June 3, the armies faced one another at Cold Harbor, the site in 1862 of the Battle

Grant proposed to "fight it out on this line if it takes all summer," but his vow was to prove costly to the Federal regiments ordered to attack Lee's entrenched soldiers outside Petersburg, Virginia. The heavy artillerymen who had been converted into infantrymen paid a heavy price in human life under Grant's command.

FIVE FORKS

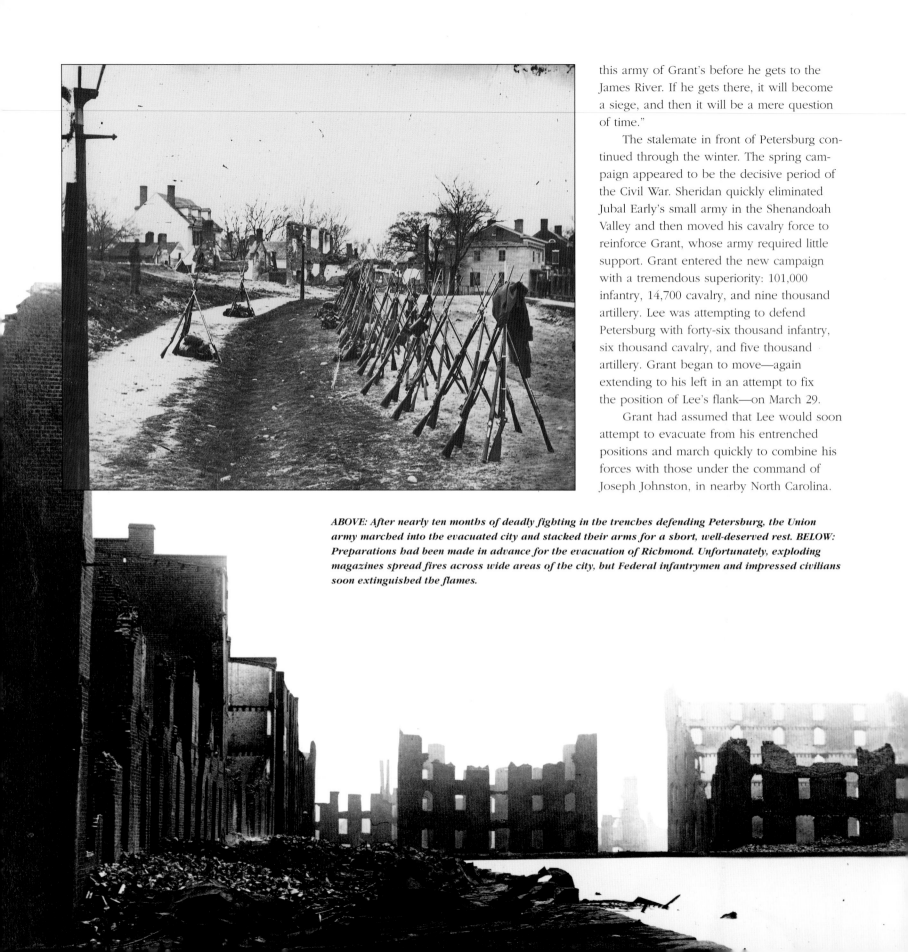

this army of Grant's before he gets to the James River. If he gets there, it will become a siege, and then it will be a mere question of time."

The stalemate in front of Petersburg continued through the winter. The spring campaign appeared to be the decisive period of the Civil War. Sheridan quickly eliminated Jubal Early's small army in the Shenandoah Valley and then moved his cavalry force to reinforce Grant, whose army required little support. Grant entered the new campaign with a tremendous superiority: 101,000 infantry, 14,700 cavalry, and nine thousand artillery. Lee was attempting to defend Petersburg with forty-six thousand infantry, six thousand cavalry, and five thousand artillery. Grant began to move—again extending to his left in an attempt to fix the position of Lee's flank—on March 29.

Grant had assumed that Lee would soon attempt to evacuate from his entrenched positions and march quickly to combine his forces with those under the command of Joseph Johnston, in nearby North Carolina.

ABOVE: After nearly ten months of deadly fighting in the trenches defending Petersburg, the Union army marched into the evacuated city and stacked their arms for a short, well-deserved rest. BELOW: Preparations had been made in advance for the evacuation of Richmond. Unfortunately, exploding magazines spread fires across wide areas of the city, but Federal infantrymen and impressed civilians soon extinguished the flames.

Bloody fighting occurred when Union divisions began their final attacks against Confederate fortifications in front of Petersburg. Many Confederate soldiers had two rifles—as a rear rank loaded the spent guns, the front rank fired devastating volleys into the Union men.

Richmond had become an arsenal during the war. The capital and government buildings were within sight of arms depots that had been abandoned.

The concentration of these two relatively large Confederate armies could present a threat to the Army of the Potomac until Sherman arrived with his army. Thus, Grant developed plans to prevent Lee's withdrawal. A large infantry flanking force was ordered to press against the Confederate side and rear, drawing them from their trenches in an open battle, and at the same time, Sheridan was ordered to move his cavalry carefully to the rear of Lee and engage the Confederates there. If Lee's divisions could not be drawn out to fight, Sheridan was to destroy secondary targets, especially the Southside and Danville Railroads, thereby blocking a potential escape route and cutting Lee's last supply line.

As at Atlanta, the railroads were targets the Confederates had to defend. Lee reacted immediately to the Union attacks by sending Pickett's division to the threatened area. He also sent all of his available cavalry to assist in the defense of his right flank and vital rear areas. Sent on a reconnaissance in force, a division of Confederate infantry struck Warren's V Corps and general fighting on the southern end of the defensive line began. Grant, sensing an opportunity to bring on a full-scale engagement in which his superior numbers would prove decisive, changed Sheridan's orders. Sheridan's new target was the Confederate rear.

One of Sheridan's cavalry divisions ran into Fitzhugh Lee's cavalry at the road junction Five Forks. Fitzhugh Lee, nephew of the commanding general, deployed his men and skirmishing began as the weather changed. Heavy rain forced Grant to halt operations for the day, but the battle was only postponed for a short period. Sheridan's cavalry found Pickett's division in entrenched positions at Five Forks and the Confederates appeared to be prepared to fight. Grant sent Sheridan infantry support—V Corps under Major General Gouverneur Warren,

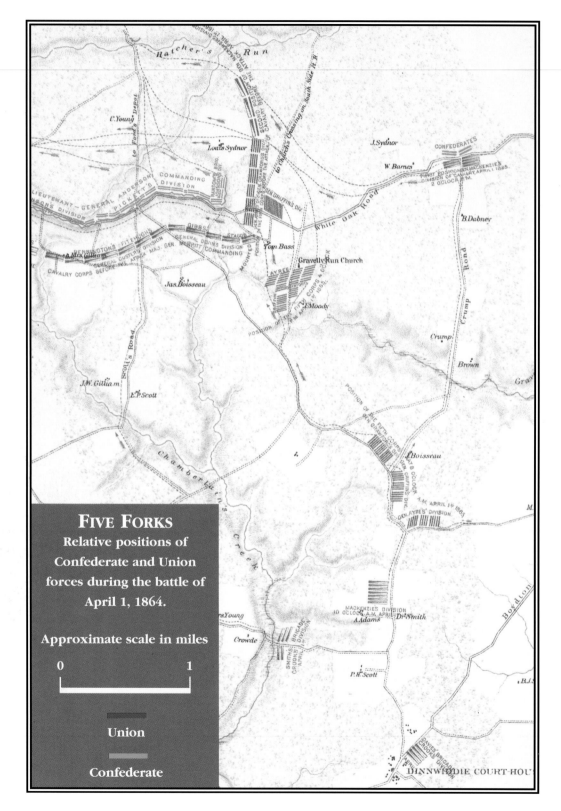

FIVE FORKS

Relative positions of Confederate and Union forces during the battle of April 1, 1864.

Approximate scale in miles

0   1

Union

Confederate

a hero of the battle of Gettysburg—for the cavalry. Sheridan had requested the services of Horatio Wright's VI Corps, a force that had served him well in the Shenandoah Valley, but Wright was too far away to be moved in the rain—especially during the night. Warren would have to do.

Lee, aggressive to the last, ordered Pickett—a general whose sole accomplishment for the Confederate war effort to this point had been leading the ill-fated attack at Gettysburg—to hold the line against Sheridan at Five Forks. The Confederate commander then sent orders to A.P. Hill and Richard Anderson to attack Warren's flank. They intended to fight hard as the rain stopped.

Sheridan, confident and full of fight, suffered from a considerable amount of overconfidence as the rain stopped and roads began to dry. He was soon made aware that Pickett's men, instead of preparing to receive a Union cavalry attack, were in the process of attacking. Pickett was managing a well-coordinated infantry and cavalry attack against the Federal cavalrymen, who were being driven slowly to the south. Less confident by this point, Sheridan called Custer's division from escort duties with the Union wagon train and with his help was able to stabilize his position as darkness fell.

Warren was also having problems in the area. One of his divisions had been sent to White Oak Road, walked into a flanking attack, and were in danger of being routed. Two divisions were hit very hard; only the

The Battle of Five Forks has been described as "The Waterloo of the Confederacy." Believing the Confederate infantry could successfully fight off any Federal cavalry attack, General Pickett attended a "shadbake" in a location where the sound of the battle did not reach him. By the time he and his generals were aware that a battle was being fought nearby, it was too late—Pickett barely escaped capture as his men were routed.

Brigadier General Stephen Dodson Ramseur (seated, right) and the brave men of the North Carolina brigade under his command defended their position against overwhelming odds on May 12, 1864, during the fighting near Spotsylvania Court House.

reserve division and Nelson Miles' divisions from II Corps were able to hold the attackers at bay. Warren assigned the responsibility for a counterattack to Brigadier General Joshua Chamberlain's brigade, and the wounded hero of the battle of Gettysburg led a second charge—as he had done in Pennsylvania—and recovered ground lost earlier in the day.

Pickett had handled the Federal cavalry roughly and Sheridan knew there was more to come on the morning of April 1, but there was also an opportunity within his dangerously exposed position. It was clear to Sheridan that Pickett was in more of an exposed position and plans were made for Warren to attack the Confederates on one side as Sheridan hit the other.

Pickett also was aware of his dangerously exposed position and began a cautious withdrawal at dawn on April 1. Sheridan sent immediate orders to Warren: the infantry must move at once. But by the time they were in their assigned positions, the Confederates were gone and Sheridan angrily planned a second plan of attack. His dismounted cavalry would be assigned the task of hitting Pickett's line and holding them in their positions as Warren's infantry struck their left flank. If Pickett's small corps could be driven to the west, Sheridan felt he could cut it off from the rest of Lee's army and destroy it. He met with Warren and reviewed the plan. As Warren later stated about the fateful meeting: "...he was convinced that I understood him," but the infantry commander would be too slow in his deployment and would earn Sheridan's disapproval.

Pickett had wisely prepared his men for the attack and bent his line back along White Oak Road to guard his otherwise exposed flank. He had deployed his forces in the best manner he could; having no evidence that a Federal attack was imminent, he accepted an invitation to lunch from Thomas Rosser, one of his cavalry commanders. Some of Rosser's

ABOVE: Grant, the commander of the entire Union army, remained in the field with his officers. This Mathew Brady photograph, taken after the battle at Spotsylvania, shows his "commander's call." RIGHT: Joshua Chamberlain may have saved the Union army from defeat on Little Round Top. Although severely wounded, Chamberlain fought valiantly again at Five Forks.

men had netted some shad that were running in a nearby river and Pickett, Rosser, and Fitzhugh Lee—on short rations like the rest of Lee's army—accepted the offer of food. Shortly prior to his departure, he was informed by one of his division commanders, Thomas Munford, that Federal cavalry had cut their contact with Anderson's corps to the east. Unfortunately, Pickett disregarded this warning and went to the riverbank to eat fish as an attack on his men developed. Like Grant at Fort Donelson, he compounded his mistake by not informing anyone of his location. And as Pickett and two of his cavalry commanders, Rosser and Fitzhugh Lee, ate shad the Federal V Corps began its attack. The missing commanders could not be locat-

LEFT: Brightly uniformed Zouaves, such as these men of the 155th Pennsylvania Infantry Regiment, dressed like French units operating in North Africa. BELOW: A uniform from a soldier in the 155th Pennsylvania Infantry Regiment. By the end of the war, the 155th Pennsylvania Infantry was one of the few units to retain the Zouave uniforms.

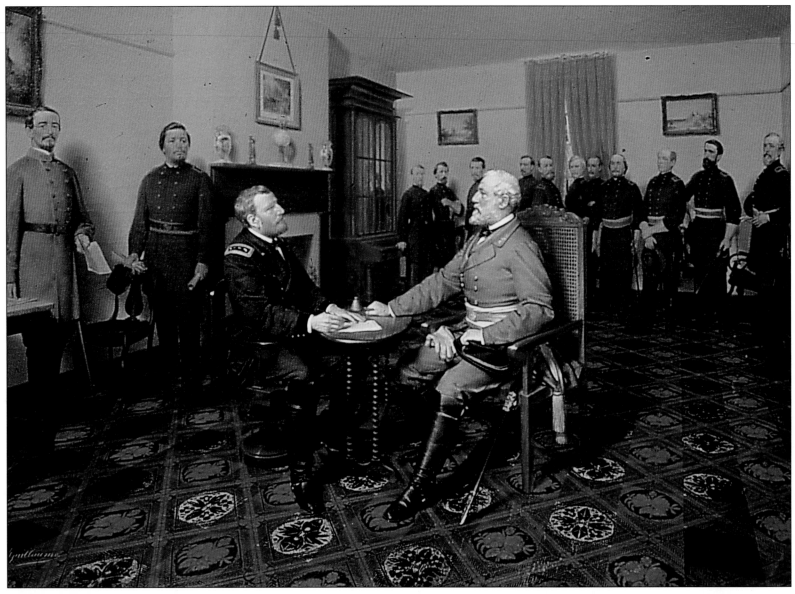

General Ulysses S. Grant met with General Robert E. Lee in Wilmer McLean's home at Appomattox Court House to sign the surrender documents that effectively ended the American Civil War.

ed and an unfortunate atmospheric effect, an "acoustic shadow," masked the sound of the battle as it started only one and a half miles from the riverbank where the missing generals were eating.

The advancing Federal infantry actually missed their opponents in their first attack, wheeled, and accidentally struck the most vulnerable portion of the opposing line, the exposed Confederate flank and rear. Sheridan was reported to be everywhere, waving his personal flag and encouraging his men to attack. The Confederate line began to collapse under the pressure from the multiple attacks that were occurring in the absence of its commander.

Pickett's first warning of the impending disaster was witnessing one of his couriers being captured by Union soldiers. Pickett himself escaped capture, arrived at the site of the battle, and saw that part of his line had been destroyed and that the remainder was being forced to the west—just as Sheridan had planned. Pickett attempted to salvage the

This photograph of Wilmer McLean's house was taken in May 1865, a month after Lee had surrendered his army to Grant.

situation, but it was too late. His entire corps was in the process of disintegrating around him as Warren's V Corps continued to attack. Meanwhile, Federal cavalry attacks swept in from both east and west to eliminate what remained of the Confederate cavalry on the battlefield.

Five Forks had been a military disaster for the Confederacy. The Southern army had lost over five thousand men as prisoners and its weakened line was scheduled to receive a general assault from Grant and his troops on the following day.

Sheridan had managed to win at Five Forks, but he was dissatisfied with the performance of Gouverneur Warren, who had led his V Corps into the rear of Pickett's line—to cut off the Confederates' retreat—

"Grant had been sleeping with one eye open and one foot out of bed for many weeks in the fear that Lee would give him the slip."

—General Horace Porter

too slowly. Sheridan relieved Warren, destroying his military career. The dismissed commander requested a court of inquiry, which was eventually held. Warren was finally vindicated in 1882—three months after his death.

Grant renewed the attack on April 2, breaking the Confederate line and forcing the defenders to the North. Lee was forced to abandon Richmond and his Petersburg line, march quickly west to Lynchburg or Danville, and join forces with Johnston—as had been anticipated by Grant. Grant had at last accomplished what he most wished for: Lee was in the open and his tired army was vulnerable. Sheridan hurried west to cut off the Confederate retreat while Grant's infantry pursued relentlessly in a running battle that lasted from April 2 through April 6. Ewell's corps was cut off, surrounded, and captured at Sayler's Creek as Confederate soldiers began to straggle and be captured. When Sheridan moved his cavalry into Appomattox Court House, directly on Lee's line of retreat, the Confederate commander realized that continued resistance was futile. He met with Grant at Wilmer McLean's house in Appomattox on April 9, 1865, and the Civil War in the east was over.

Joseph Johnston surrendered to Sherman on April 26 and Kirby Smith surrendered the last remaining Confederate force in the west on May 26, personally signing the surrender document on June 2.

Lee's excellent defensive line had held Grant's army at bay for months, but once Sheridan was able to defeat Pickett at Five Forks the reduced companies holding the entrenched Confederate positions at Petersburg were unable to resist Grant's overwhelming forces on the day following the battle. Five Forks was the critical point in the Petersburg campaign, and this crucial battle led to the rapid collapse of the entire Confederacy.

The Civil War was over at last.

SUGGESTED READING

Fort Donelson

Cooling, Frank. "West Virginians at Fort Donelson, February 1862," *West Virginia History*, vol. XXVII, no. 2. January 1967.

Force, M.F. *From Fort Henry to Corinth: Campaigns of the Civil War Series*. New York: Charles Scribner's Sons, 1881.

Phillips, David L. *Tiger John: The Rebel Who Burned Chambersburg*. Gauley Mount Press, 1993.

United States General Staff School. *Fort Henry and Fort Donelson—1862*. Fort Leavenworth, Kans.: U.S. General Services School, 1923.

Walke, Henry. "The Western Flotilla at Fort Donelson," *The War of the Rebellion*, vol. 7. 1893.

Wallace, Lew. "The Capture of Fort Donelson," *Battles and Leaders*. Ed. Ned Bradford. New York: Penguin Group, Meridian Books, 1989.

Pea Ridge

Mulligan, James A. "The Siege of Lexington," *Battles and Leaders*, vol. 1.. Ed. Robert U. Johnson and Clarence C. Buel. 1887.

Sigel, Franz. "The Flanking Column at Wilson's Creek," *Battles and Leaders*, vol. 1. Ed. Robert U. Johnson and Clarence C. Buel. 1887.

_____. "The Pea Ridge Campaign," *Battles and Leaders*, vol. 1. Ed. Robert U. Johnson and Clarence C. Buel. 1887.

Snead, Thomas L. "The First Year of the War in Missouri," *Battles and Leaders*. Ed. Robert U. Johnson and Clarence C. Buel, vol. 1. 1887.

United States War Department. "Battle of Pea Ridge, or Elkhorn, Ark.," *The War of the Rebellion*, series 1, vol. 8. 1893.

Antietam

Cox, Jacob D. "The Battle of Antietam," *Battles and Leaders*. Ed. Ned Bradford. New York: Penguin Group, Meridian Books, 1989.

Hill, Daniel H. "The Battle of South Mountain, or Boonsboro," *Battles and Leaders,* vol. 1. Ed. Robert U. Johnson and Clarence C. Buel. 1887.

Longstreet, James. "The Invasion of Maryland," *Battles and Leaders*. Ed. Ned Bradford. New York: Penguin Group, Meridian Books, 1989.

United States War Department. "The Maryland Campaign," *The War of the Rebellion*, series 1, vol. 19. 1893.

Vicksburg

Grant, Ulysses S. "The Vicksburg Campaign," *Battles and Leaders*. Ed. Ned Bradford. New York: Penguin Group, Meridian Books, 1989.

Lockett, S.H. "The Defense of Vicksburg," *Battles and Leaders*, vol. 3. Ed. Robert U. Johnson and Clarence C. Buel. 1887.

Morgan, George W. "The Assault on Chickasaw Bluffs," *Battles and Leaders*, vol. 3. Ed. Robert U. Johnson and Clarence C. Buel. 1887.

Soley, James R. "Naval Operations in the Vicksburg Campaign," *Battles and Leaders*, vol. 3. Ed. Robert U. Johnson and Clarence C. Buel. 1887.

United States War Department. "General Reports—Vicksburg," *The War of the Rebellion*, vols. 24 and 25. 1893.

Gettysburg

Alexander, E. Porter. "The Great Charge and Artillery Fighting at Gettysburg," *Battles and Leaders*. Ed. Ned Bradford. New York: Penguin Group, Meridian Books, 1989.

Hunt, Henry J. "The First Day at Gettysburg," *Battles and Leaders*. Ed. Ned Bradford. New York: Penguin Group, Meridian Books, 1989.

_____. "The Second Day at Gettysburg," *Battles and Leaders*. Ed. Ned Bradford. New York: Penguin Group, Meridian Books, 1989.

_____. "The Third Day at Gettysburg," *Battles and Leaders*. Ed. Ned Bradford. New York: Penguin Group, Meridian Books, 1989.

Imboden, John D. "The Confederate Retreat from Gettysburg," *Battles and Leaders*, vol. 3. Ed. Robert U. Johnson and Clarence C. Buel. 1887.

Kershaw, J.B. "Kershaw's Brigade at Gettysburg," *Battles and Leaders*, vol. 3. Ed. Robert U. Johnson and Clarence C. Buel. 1887.

Longstreet, James. "Lee's Invasion of Pennsylvania," *Battles and Leaders*, vol. 3. Ed. Robert U. Johnson and Clarence C. Buel. 1887.

Melcher, H.S. "The 20th Maine at Little Round Top," *Battles and Leaders*, vol. 3. Ed. Robert U. Johnson and Clarence C. Buel. 1887.

United States War Department. "Gettysburg," The War of the Rebellion, series 1, vol. 27. 1897.

Monocacy

Early, Jubal. "Early's March to Washington in 1864," *Battles and Leaders*. Ed. Ned Bradford. New York: Penguin Group, Meridian Books, 1989.

_____. *War Memoirs*. Ed. Frank Vandiver. Bloomington, Ind.: Indiana University Press, 1960.

Gordon, John B. *Reminiscences of the Civil War*. New York: Charles Scribner's Sons, 1903.

United States War Department. "Monocacy," *The War of the Rebellion*, series 1, vol. 27. 1897.

Peachtree Creek

Cox, Jacob D. *Atlanta*. New York: Charles Scribner's Sons, 1882.

Hood, John B. "The Defense of Atlanta," *Battles and Leaders*. Ed. Ned Bradford. New York: Penguin Group, Meridian Books, 1989.

Howard, Oliver O. "The Struggle for Atlanta," *Battles and Leaders*. Ed. Ned Bradford. New York: Penguin Group, Meridian Books, 1989.

Johnston, Joseph E. "Opposing Sherman's Advance to Atlanta," *Battles and Leaders*, vol. 4. Ed. Robert U. Johnson and Clarence C. Buel. 1887.

Sherman, William T. "The Grand Strategy of the Last Year of the War," *Battles and Leaders*, vol. 4. Ed. Robert U. Johnson and Clarence C. Buel. 1887.

United States War Department. "Atlanta Campaign," *The War of the Rebellion*, series 1, vol. 38. 1893.

Five Forks

Porter, Horace. *Campaigning with Grant*. New York: The Century Co., 1897.

_____. "Five Forks and the Pursuit of Lee," *Battles and Leaders*, vol. 4. Ed. Robert U. Johnson and Clarence C. Buel. 1887.

Sheridan, Philip H. *Personal Memoirs of P.H. Sheridan*, vol. 2. New York: Jenkins and McCowan, 1888.

Sulivane, Clement. "The Evacuation," *Battles and Leaders*, vol. 4. Ed. Robert U. Johnson and Clarence C. Buel. 1887.

Tremain, Henry E. *Last Hours of Sheridan's Cavalry*. New York: Bonnell, Silver & Bowers, 1904.

PHOTO CREDITS

AP/Wide World Photos: p. 120 top, **Archive Photos:** p. 52 top, © **Christopher Bain:** pp. 14, 28, 38, 54, 64, 84, 94 bottom left, 95 bottom, 98, 112, **The Bettman Archive:** pp. 11 top, 13, 17, 18 right, 19 left, 22 bottom, 24, 25, 26, 30, 31, 32 right, 33 both, 44 left, 45 bottom, 53, 58 both, 63 top, 70 both, 71 top, 81, 82, 88 right, 89, 92 all, 94 bottom right, 101 right, 105 middle and right, 106 right, 107 top, 108 bottom, 111, 113 inset, 117 top, 123, **Courtesy of the Anne S.K. Brown Military Collection, Brown University Library:** p. 29 inset, **Brown Brothers:** pp. 19 right, 109, **Eleanor S. Brockenbrough Library, The Museum of the Confederacy, Richmond, VA:** p. 76 bottom, © **Hal E. Gieseking:** p. 50 bottom, **Battle Diagrams by Bob Keene:** pp. 21, 34, 51, 78, **Frank Leslie's Illustrated Newspaper:** pp. 15 background, 29 background, 39 background, 55 background, 65 background, 85 background, 99 background, 113 background, **Library of Congress:** pp. 8–9, 39 inset, 40–41 bottom, 45 top, 49, 50 top, 52 bottom, 55 inset, 57 both, 61, 63 bottom, 65 inset, 68, 75, 76, 83, 107 bottom, 114, 116 both, 117 bottom, © **Eric Long Photography:** p. 97, © **National Portrait Gallery/Art Resource:** p. 101 left, **Northwind Picture Archives:** pp. 22 top, 32 left, 37, 67, 72, 96, 105 left, © **Aloysius T. O'Donnell:** p. 88 left, **Courtesy of the Pejepscot Historical Society, Brunswick, ME:** p. 120 bottom, **Courtesy Beverly R. Robinson Collection/U.S. Naval Academy Museum, Annapolis, MD:** pp. 23, 40 top, 60, **Stock Montage:** p. 27, **Superstock:** pp. 85 inset, 99 inset; AKG Berlin: p. 15 inset; H. Lanks: p. 122, © **Don Troiani:** pp. 90, 94 top, 121 bottom, **Painting by Don Troiani; Photograph courtesy Historical Art Prints, Southbury, CT:** pp. 36, 48, 62, 66, 71 bottom, 73, 74, 77, 80, 93, 103, 110, 119, **UPI/Bettman:** p. 11 bottom, **Courtesy of the Valentine Museum/Cook Collection:** pp. 10, 19 middle, 44 right, **Courtesy of the Virginia Military Institute:** p. 87 all, **Courtesy VMI Public Relations Office; Painting by Benjamin West Klinedinst depicting the charge of VMI cadets at the Battle of New Market; (the mural is fixed to the wall of VMI's Jackson Memorial Hall; from THE CIVIL WAR: SHENANDOAH IN FLAMES, photograph by Michael Latil.) © 1987 Time-Life Books, Inc.:** p. 86, **Washington Government Printing Office:** pp. 16, 17, 20, 35 top, 46, 56, 69, 91, 100, 104, 118, **Courtesy of the West Point Museum, United States Military Academy, West Point, NY:** p. 12, **Courtesy of the Western History Collection, University of Oklahoma Library:** p. 47, **Frank and Marie-Terese Wood Print Collections, Alexandria, VA:** pp. 59, 106 left, 108 top

INDEX